I0606102

The Greek Kitchen

The Greek Kitchen

Vefa Alexiadou

▽ VEGAN

▼ VEGETARIAN

✲ GLUTEN-FREE

◍ DAIRY-FREE

⬠ NUT-FREE

❺ 5 INGREDIENTS OR FEWER

◷ 30 MINUTES OR LESS

❶ ONE-POT

Introduction

Greek cuisine is one of the world's most enduring and beloved food traditions—delicious, generous, and rooted in a culture where cooking is about far more than just feeding the body. It is a cuisine shaped by sun-drenched landscapes, a rich coastline, and centuries of history, trade, and cultural exchange. At the heart of this tradition is Vefa Alexiadou, widely recognized as the leading authority on Greek cookery. Her life's work documenting and preserving the authentic recipes of her homeland has been instrumental in bringing Greek food to a wider audience, both in Greece and abroad.

This book brings together 75 of the very best authentic recipes from across Greece, each carefully chosen to be accessible to the home cook without compromising on authenticity. Whether it's a hearty fish soup, a celebratory lamb dish, or a table full of classic meze, each recipe reflects the values that Vefa so passionately championed: good ingredients, thoughtful preparation, and food made to be shared.

Greek food is often associated with bold, sun-ripened ingredients—sweet tomatoes, tangy feta, plump olives, and aromatic herbs—all brought together with the rich, peppery notes of extra virgin olive oil. But behind these familiar ingredients lies a deep and diverse culinary heritage. From the mountainous villages of the north to the island kitchens of the Aegean, Greek cooking encompasses a wide range of regional styles and techniques, many of which are included in this collection.

The Greek larder is simple, yet full of possibilities. Pulses such as lentils and giant butter beans form the basis of countless hearty dishes, while seasonal vegetables are baked, stewed, roasted, or turned into pies. Herbs are used liberally, bringing freshness and fragrance to even the simplest recipes. Meanwhile, spices such as cinnamon and allspice may occasionally make an unexpected appearance, especially in dishes with influences from the Levant and Asia Minor.

The Greek Kitchen is your gateway to cooking Greek food as it is cooked in homes and village kitchens across the country—faithfully, simply, and with passion. Whether you're discovering these dishes for the first time or returning to well-loved classics, the recipes in this book offer a window into one of the most enduring food cultures in the world. With the guidance of Vefa Alexiadou, and an emphasis on fresh ingredients and traditional methods, this is Greek cookery at its finest—made for real kitchens and real cooks.

Mezedes

Rice-stuffed Grape Leaves

Serves 8
Preparation time 1 hour
Cooking time 35–40 minutes

1 lb 2 oz (500 g) **grape (vine) leaves**, fresh or preserved in brine

2 cups (175 g / 6 oz) finely chopped **scallions** (spring onions)

2 large **onions**, chopped

salt and **pepper**

2½ cups (500 g / 1 lb 2 oz) **medium-grain rice**

½ cup (25 g / 1 oz) chopped **fresh parsley**

½ cup (15 g / ½ oz) chopped **fresh dill**

2 cups (450 ml / 16 fl oz) **olive oil**

4 tablespoons **pine nuts** (optional)

4 tablespoons **currants** (optional)

2½ cups (600 ml / 1 pint) **boiling water**

5 tablespoons freshly squeezed **lemon juice**

Tzatziki (p 42) or **plain yogurt**, to serve

Rinse the grape (vine) leaves and trim off the stems, if necessary. Bring a pan of water to a boil, add the leaves, a few at a time, and blanch briefly, then drain, and let cool.

Spread out some of the leaves to cover the base of a large, wide, heavy pan.

Put the scallions (spring onions) and onions into a colander, sprinkle with a little salt, and rub with your fingers. Rinse with a little water and drain, then squeeze out as much liquid as possible.

Combine the rice, onions, herbs, half the oil, the pine nuts, and currants, if using, in a bowl and season with salt and pepper.

Lay a leaf out flat on the work surface, shiny side down. Put about 1 tablespoon of the rice mixture at the stem end in the middle, fold the sides over the filling, and loosely roll up into a neat parcel. Continue making grape leaf parcels until all the ingredients have been used. Arrange the stuffed leaves in the lined pan, side by side, seam side down. (You may have to make more than one layer.) Carefully pour the remaining oil, the boiling water, and lemon juice into the pan. Invert a heavy plate on the top of the parcels to prevent them from opening during cooking.

Cover the pan and bring to a boil, then reduce the heat, and simmer for 35–40 minutes, until all the water has been absorbed. Remove from the heat, place a dish towel or some paper towels between the pan and the lid to absorb the steam, and let cool. Transfer to a serving platter. Serve with Tzatziki or plain yogurt.

Note: The parsley can be replaced with chopped fresh mint and the dill with chopped fennel fronds.

Cuttlefish in Wine

Serves 4
Preparation time 15 minutes
Cooking time 1¾ hours

2¼ lb (1 kg) **cuttlefish**, cleaned (see Notes)

⅔ cup (150 ml / ¼ pint) **olive oil**

2½ lb (1 kg) **onions**, thinly sliced

6 **garlic cloves**, finely chopped

3 tablespoons **tomato paste** (purée)

1 cup (250 ml / 8 fl oz) **white wine**

2 **bay leaves**

3 **allspice berries**

10 **black peppercorns**

½ teaspoon **sugar**

If the cuttlefish are small, leave them whole. Cut large cuttlefish crosswise into rings. Rinse and drain well.

Heat the oil in a heavy pan. Add the onions and garlic and cook over low heat, stirring occasionally, for about 5 minutes, until softened and translucent. Add the cuttlefish, partially cover, and cook until all the liquid has evaporated.

Combine the tomato paste (purée) and wine, stir well, and pour the mixture over the cuttlefish. Add the bay leaves, allspice berries, peppercorns, and sugar. Stir well, cover, and simmer over medium heat for about 1½ hours, until the cuttlefish is tender and the sauce has reduced and cooked down almost to the oil.

Notes: To clean cuttlefish, pull off the heads; the innards, including the ink sac, will come away with them. (If you want to reserve the ink sac, cut it away from the intestines and place in a bowl of cold water.) Using a sharp knife, cut off the tentacles from just above the eyes. Squeeze out the beak and discard, together with the rest of the head. Pull out the hard white cuttlebone. Rinse thoroughly under running water and peel off the translucent membrane.

Squid or octopus can be used instead of cuttlefish. If using squid, follow the recipe above. If using octopus, it should first be blanched in a mixture of water and vinegar for a couple of minutes, then peel off the skin. Cut it into bite-size pieces and proceed as for the cuttlefish. As octopus requires longer to cook, it may be necessary to add more water. Simmer until the octopus is tender and the sauce has reduced.

Fried Squid

⬠

Serves 4
Preparation time 1 hour 10 minutes (including standing)
Cooking time 15 minutes

2¼ lb (1 kg) small **squid**, cleaned (see Note)

vegetable oil, for frying

lemon wedges, to garnish

Tzatziki (p 42), **Eggplant (Aubergine) Dip** (p 44), or **Taramosalata** (p 47), to serve

FOR THE BATTER

1 cup (120 g / 4 oz) **all-purpose (plain) flour**

salt and **pepper**

1 tablespoon **olive oil**

1 cup (250 ml / 8 fl oz) **beer** or **club soda** (soda water)

2 **egg whites**

For the batter, sift the flour with a pinch of salt and pepper into a bowl. Make a well in the center and pour in the oil and beer or club soda. Gradually stir into the flour until a smooth, thin batter forms. Avoid overmixing. Add a little more flour, if a thicker batter is required. Let stand for about 1 hour.

Meanwhile, rinse the squid under running water and drain. Leave finger-length squid whole, otherwise cut them into thick rings.

When ready to use the batter, beat the egg whites until they form soft peaks, then gradually fold into the batter.

Heat the oil in a deep-fryer to 400°F (200°C).

Dip the squid into the batter and let the excess drain off. Deep-fry the squid or squid rings, a few at a time, for a few minutes until light golden brown. Remove with a slotted spoon and drain on paper towels.

Arrange on a platter, sprinkle with salt, garnish with lemon wedges, and serve immediately with Tzatziki, Eggplant (Aubergine) Dip or Taramosalata.

Note: To clean squid, pull off the heads; the innards, including the ink sac, will come away with them. (If you want to reserve the ink sac, cut it away from the intestines and place in a bowl of cold water.) Using a sharp knife, cut off the tentacles from just above the eyes. Squeeze out the beak and discard, together with the rest of the head. Pull out the translucent quill from the body sac. Rinse thoroughly under running water and peel off the translucent membrane.

Mixed Lamb Skewers

Serves 8–10
Preparation time 6 hours (including soaking)
Cooking time 1 hour

organ meats (offal) of 2 spring lambs: 4 kidneys, 2 livers, and 2 hearts

2 **lamb's sweetbreads**, soaked in several changes of cold water for 5 hours and drained

pinch of **dried oregano**

salt and **pepper**

3¼ lb (1.5 kg) spring **lamb's intestines**

about 4 cups (about 1 liter / 1¾ pints) **red wine vinegar**

3 large **lamb's cauls**, soaked in water to soften and cut into medium-size pieces

olive oil, for brushing

radishes and **scallions** (spring onions), sliced, to garnish

lettuce leaves, to serve

Remove and discard any tubes, cores, and membranes from the kidneys, livers, hearts, and lungs and rinse well. Sprinkle with the oregano and salt and pepper and set aside.

Wash the intestines carefully and thoroughly but do not cut into pieces. Place in a bowl, pour over vinegar to cover, and set aside for 30 minutes. Rinse with plenty of cold running water and drain.

Thread the organ meats onto three long skewers and wrap the cauls around them. Secure them to the skewers by winding the intestines up and around, so that they cover the whole skewer. Brush with olive oil and chill in the refrigerator until ready to cook. (You can also wrap and freeze them. When ready to cook, thaw fully first.)

Preheat the broiler (grill) or light the charcoal on a barbecue. Brush with oil and broil (grill) or, preferably, grill over charcoal, brushing frequently with oil and turning, for about 1 hour, or until browned all over and no pink juices flow when the meat is pricked with a fork.

Make a bed of lettuce on a platter and top with the meat. Garnish with radishes and scallions (spring onions) and serve hot.

Note: You can also bake the skewers (*kokoretsi*) in a preheated oven at 400°F (200°C / Gas Mark 6) and then brown both sides under the broiler (grill).

Broiled or Fried Peppers

Serves 4
Preparation time 15 minutes
Cooking time 10 minutes

1 lb 2 oz (500 g) long mild green or red **peppers**

1 long hot **green chile pepper** (optional)

3 tablespoons **olive oil** (optional)

salt

red wine vinegar

FOR THE OIL-VINEGAR DRESSING

2 parts **olive oil**

1 part **red wine vinegar**

salt and **pepper**

pinch of **dried oregano** or **mustard powder** (optional)

For the oil-vinegar dressing, put the oil, vinegar, and salt and pepper to taste into a screw-top jar, fasten the lid, and shake vigorously until thoroughly blended. Flavor the dressing with oregano or mustard powder, depending on the occasion. You could also add any other fresh or dried herb you like.

Make a slit in each pepper to release the steam while cooking. Grill over charcoal or fry in the oil, turning frequently, for about 10 minutes, until browned on all sides.

Transfer the peppers to a deep plate, cover with plastic wrap (cling film), and let stand for a few minutes until cool enough to handle. While they are still hot, peel off the skins and sprinkle them with salt and oil-vinegar dressing to taste. If you fried the peppers, do not add dressing, but sprinkle with 2–3 tablespoons of the frying oil, salt, and red wine vinegar to taste. The chile pepper will give the dish a slightly spicy flavor and you can use more of them, if you like. Peppers prepared this way taste better the second day and are especially delicious with ouzo or retsina.

Garlic-stuffed Zucchini

Serves 6
Preparation time 30 minutes
Cooking time 1½ hours

12 small **zucchini** (courgettes), about 2¼ lb (1 kg) total weight

18 **garlic cloves**, thinly sliced

1 cup (50 g / 2 oz) chopped **fresh parsley**

1 teaspoon **paprika**

⅔ cup (150 ml / ¼ pint) **olive oil**

salt and **pepper**

12 small, thin slices **feta cheese**

2–3 tablespoons **all-purpose (plain) flour**

Trim the zucchini and, using a sharp knife, make 4 evenly spaced slits lengthwise along each one, making sure not to cut right through the ends.

Preheat the oven to 350°F (180°C / Gas Mark 4).

Combine the garlic, parsley, paprika, and half of the oil in a bowl and season with salt and pepper. Rub the garlic mixture into every slit in each zucchini, pressing with your thumb.

Arrange the zucchini side by side in a single layer in an ovenproof dish and insert a slice of feta cheese into the uppermost slit. Pour ½ cup (120 ml / 4 fl oz) water and the remaining oil over the zucchini and dust with a little flour. Cover the dish with aluminum foil and bake for about 1½ hours, or until the zucchini are soft and the sauce has reduced. Serve hot or at room temperature.

Fried Whitebait Pie

Serves 4
Preparation time 45 minutes (including salting)
Cooking time 20 minutes

1 lb 2 oz (500 g) **whitebait** or other **tiny fish**

1 **onion**, thinly sliced

salt and **pepper**

all-purpose (plain) flour, to coat

½ cup (120 ml / 4 fl oz) **olive oil**

Rinse the fish, drain, and dry on paper towels. Put the onion in a colander, sprinkle with a little salt, and set aside for 30 minutes. Rinse and squeeze out excess liquid. Combine the fish and onion in a bowl, season with salt and pepper, add enough flour to coat, and toss well.

Heat the oil in a heavy, nonstick skillet or frying pan and add the fish, spreading them out to cover the base of the pan and pressing them with a spatula so that they stick to each other. The layer of fish should be no thicker than 1 inch (2.5 cm), so you may need to cook in batches. Cook over medium heat for 8–10 minutes, until set, then turn over. (The easiest way to do this is to invert a plate over the pan and, holding the two together, turn the layer of fish onto the plate. Slide the fish back into the pan to cook the second side.)

Cook for 8 minutes more, until lightly browned. Serve immediately. This is an excellent meze with ouzo.

ΟΥΖΟ

Sardines in Oil and Oregano

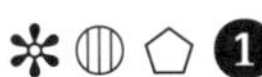

Serves 4
Preparation time 30 minutes
Cooking time 20–30 minutes

2¼ lb (1 kg) **fresh sardines** or **anchovies**

½ cup (120 ml / 4 fl oz) **olive oil**

5–6 **garlic cloves**, sliced

2 tablespoons **red wine vinegar**

pinch of **dried oregano**

salt and **pepper**

Scale the sardines by running one hand from tail to head while holding the fish by the tail under cold running water. Alternatively, put them in cold water to cover and rub with your fingers to remove the scales. Anchovies do not require scaling.

Cut off and discard the heads of the sardines. To remove the guts, gently squeeze the belly of each fish, hold down the guts with a knife as they are exposed, and pull them out. To clean anchovies, pinch the head of a fish between your thumb and forefinger and pull it off—the guts should come away with it. Cut off the tail, pinch all along the top edge of the fish, and pull out the backbone—it should come away easily. Repeat with all the remaining anchovies. Rinse the fish, drain, and pat dry with paper towels.

Heat the oil in a large heavy skillet or frying pan over high heat. Add the garlic and cook, stirring constantly, for about 1 minute. Put the fish in a single layer to cover the base of the skillet or frying pan, sprinkle with the vinegar and oregano, and season with salt and pepper. Cook over high heat for about 20 minutes, until the liquid has reduced. Serve hot or at room temperature. Alternatively, arrange the fish in a single layer with all the other ingredients in an ovenproof dish and bake in a preheated oven at 400°F (200°C / Gas Mark 6) for 20–30 minutes, or until the sardines are cooked and the liquid has reduced.

Stuffed Mussels

⬠

Serves 4
Preparation time 30 minutes
Cooking time 10 minutes

4½ lb (2 kg) **mussels**

2 tablespoons finely chopped **fresh parsley**

4 **garlic cloves**, finely chopped

¾ cup (40 g / 1½ oz) fresh **bread crumbs**

5 tablespoons **grated kefalotyri** or **pecorino cheese**

4 tablespoons **olive oil**

salt and **pepper**

lemon wedges, to garnish

buttered toast, to serve

Scrub the mussels under cold running water and pull off the beards. Discard any with damaged shells or that do not shut immediately when sharply tapped.

Bring 2 cups (450 ml / 16 fl oz) water to a boil in a pan. Add the mussels and simmer for 8 minutes. Drain and discard any mussels that remain shut.

Preheat the broiler (grill).

Combine the parsley, garlic, bread crumbs, cheese, and half the oil in a bowl and season with salt and pepper. Discard the empty half shells. Put 1 tablespoon of the cheese mixture into each half shell and put the shells, filled side up, in a flameproof dish.

Broil (grill) for 7–8 minutes, or until the topping is lightly browned. Drizzle the remaining oil over them and garnish with lemon wedges. Serve hot straight from the dish, accompanied by buttered toast.

Pumpkin Fritters

Makes 20–25 fritters
Preparation time 3 hours (including salting and chilling)
Cooking time 15 minutes

2¼ lb (1 kg) **pumpkin** or other **yellow winter squash**, peeled and grated

salt and **pepper**

1⅔ cups (150 g / 5 oz) finely chopped **spinach**

3–4 fresh **garlic stems**, finely chopped, or 1 small **garlic clove**, finely chopped

½ cup (50 g / 2 oz) finely chopped **scallions** (spring onions)

5 tablespoons finely chopped **fresh dill**

5 tablespoons finely chopped **fennel fronds**

4 tablespoons finely chopped **fresh mint**

3 **eggs**, lightly beaten

2¼ cups (250 g / 9 oz) **crumbled feta** or other **mild cheese**

pinch of **ground cumin** (optional)

pinch of **ground cinnamon** (optional)

scant 1½ cups (100 g / 3½ oz) dry **bread crumbs**

all-purpose (plain) flour, for coating

olive oil, for frying

Tzatziki (p 42), **Garlic Sauce** (p 45), or **Eggplant (Aubergine) Dip** (p 44), to serve

Put the grated pumpkin or squash into a colander, sprinkle with a little salt, and let drain for 1–2 hours. Squeeze out the moisture with your hands.

Combine the spinach, garlic, scallions (spring onions), and herbs in a large bowl, sprinkle with salt and pepper, and knead the mixture lightly to bruise it. Add the drained pumpkin, eggs, cheese, and spices, if using, then gradually mix in the bread crumbs until the mixture is soft and pliable. Chill in the refrigerator for 30 minutes.

Shape the pumpkin mixture into large round patties, coat them with flour, and flatten with the palms of your hands. Pour olive oil into a heavy skillet or frying pan to a depth of 1 inch (2.5 cm) and heat. Fry the patties in batches over medium heat for about 5 minutes, or until they are lightly browned on both sides. Remove with a spatula and drain on paper towels. These fritters are delicious served either hot or cold, accompanied by Tzatziki, Garlic Sauce, or Eggplant (Aubergine) Dip.

Fried Salt Cod with Garlic Sauce

Makes 35–40 pieces
Preparation time 20¼ hours (including soaking and resting)
Cooking time 15–20 minutes

2¼ lb (1 kg) **salt cod**

vegetable oil, for deep-frying

Garlic sauce (p 45), to serve

FOR THE BATTER

1 cup (120 g / 4 oz) **all-purpose (plain) flour**

1 tablespoon **olive oil**

1 cup (250 ml / 8 fl oz) **beer** or **club soda** (soda water)

salt and **pepper**

1 **egg white**, whisked to soft peaks

Remove the skin from the cod and cut the flesh into large pieces. Put the pieces in a bowl, pour in water to cover, and let soak for 12–24 hours, changing the water 3 or 4 times.

Meanwhile, make the batter. Put the flour, olive oil, and beer or club soda into a food processor, season with salt and pepper, and process for 1 minute. Set aside for 1 hour.

Drain the fish and pat dry with paper towels. Remove the bones and cut the fish into bite-size pieces.

Heat the vegetable oil in a deep-fryer to 350–375°F (180–190°C).

Fold the egg white into the batter. Dip the pieces of cod into the batter, one at a time, and deep-fry in the hot oil until golden brown. Serve hot, accompanied by Garlic sauce.

Peppers with Sausages

Serves 6
Preparation time 1¼ hours (including salting)
Cooking time 35 minutes

3¼ lb (1.5 kg) **eggplants** (aubergines)

2¼ lb (1 kg) **tomatoes**, peeled and coarsely chopped

⅓ cup (80 ml / 3 fl oz) **olive oil**

1 lb 2 oz (500 g) long mild **green peppers**, seeded and sliced

1 lb 2 oz (500 g) spicy rustic **sausages**, thickly sliced

salt and **pepper**

Slice the eggplants (aubergines) into ½-inch (1-cm) thick rounds. Sprinkle with salt and let drain in a colander for 1 hour.

Meanwhile, process the tomatoes to a purée in a food processor. Rinse the eggplant rounds and squeeze out excess water.

Heat half the olive oil in a large skillet or frying pan. Add the eggplants and peppers and cook for 10–15 minutes, until lightly browned, then remove from the heat.

Meanwhile, cook the sausages in a nonstick skillet or frying pan over medium heat until they have released their fat. Drain and discard the fat.

Heat the remaining olive oil in the same pan and return the sausages to the pan with the tomatoes. Simmer for about 20 minutes, until the sauce has thickened.

Meanwhile, preheat the oven to 350°F (180°C / Gas Mark 4). Remove the sausages with a slotted spoon and pile in the center of an ovenproof platter. Arrange the eggplants and peppers around the sausages and spoon the remaining sauce on top. Season with pepper, cover with aluminum foil, and bake for about 15 minutes. Serve hot.

Stuffed Leeks with Egg-lemon Sauce

Serves 4
Preparation time 1 hour (including cooling)
Cooking time 1½ hours

6–7 large **thick leeks**, white part only, 8–10 inches (20–25 cm) long

⅔ cup (150 ml / ¼ pint) **olive oil**

1 **small leek**, finely chopped

14 oz (400 g) **ground (minced) pork**

⅓ cup (65 g / 2½ oz) **short-grain rice**

¼ teaspoon **ground cumin**

4 tablespoons finely chopped **fresh parsley**

2 tablespoons finely chopped **fresh mint**

salt and **pepper**

2 cups (450 ml / 16 fl oz) **boiling water**

2 **eggs**

4 tablespoons freshly squeezed **lemon juice**

Remove and discard the outer layer of each thick leek. Blanch in boiling water for 5 minutes to soften, then drain. Carefully cut each leek lengthwise to the center, separate the layers, open, and flatten.

Heat 5 tablespoons of the olive oil in a pan. Add the chopped leek and cook over low heat, stirring occasionally, for 3 minutes. Stir in the pork and cook, stirring occasionally and breaking up the meat, until it begins to brown. Stir in the rice, cumin, parsley, mint, and ½ cup (120 ml / 4 fl oz) water, season with salt and pepper, and simmer until the water is absorbed. Remove the pan from the heat and let cool.

Place a tablespoon of the pork mixture at one corner of each piece of leek and fold the other corner over it to form a triangle. Then fold the triangle over and over on itself to the end of the strip. Arrange the stuffed leeks (*sarmadakia*) side by side in a pan and pour the remaining oil over them. Place a plate slightly smaller than the width of the pan directly on top of the stuffed leeks. Pour in the boiling water, cover, and simmer for 1 hour.

Beat the eggs with the lemon juice in a bowl, then beat in a ladleful of the hot pan juices. Pour the mixture over the stuffed leeks and shake the pan to distribute. Remove from the heat and serve hot.

Drunken Pork

  1

Serves 6
Preparation time 10 minutes
Cooking time 25 minutes

1 lb 2 oz (500 g) boneless **pork loin**, cut into bite-size pieces
2 tablespoons **Dijon mustard**
4 tablespoons **olive oil**
2 **garlic cloves**, thinly sliced
1 cup (250 ml / 8 fl oz) **dry red wine**
1 cup (250 ml / 8 fl oz) **tomato juice**
½ teaspoon **cayenne pepper**
¼ teaspoon **dried oregano**
¼ teaspoon **ground allspice**
salt and **pepper**
trahana, to serve

Toss the pork in a bowl with the mustard until coated on all sides.

Heat the oil in a heavy skillet or frying pan. Add the garlic and pork and cook over medium heat, stirring frequently, for about 10 minutes, until the meat is lightly browned.

Stir in the wine, a little at a time, and cook over high heat until it has evaporated. Add the tomato juice, cayenne pepper, oregano, and allspice and season with salt and pepper. Simmer for about 10 minutes, until the meat is tender and the sauce has thickened. Serve immediately, with trahana and red wine.

Halloumi Bruschetta with Griddled Tomato Salsa

Serves 4
Preparation time 10 minutes
Cooking time 20–25 minutes

olive oil, for brushing

1 medium **eggplant** (aubergine), sliced into 8 rounds

9 oz (250 g) **halloumi**, cut into 8 slices

good-quality **balsamic vinegar**, for drizzling

GRIDDLED TOMATO SALSA

8 **baby plum tomatoes**

2 **garlic cloves**, crushed

½ **red onion**, finely chopped

few **Greek basil sprigs**, chopped

few **mint sprigs**, chopped

juice of ½ **lemon**

1 tablespoon **olive oil**

salt and **pepper**

Brush a ridged griddle pan with olive oil and place over medium heat. When hot, add the eggplant (aubergine) slices and grill for 2–3 minutes on each side, or until tender, golden, and attractively striped (if the pan is not large, you may have to do this in batches). Remove and drain on paper towels. Keep warm.

Make the griddled tomato salsa: grill the tomatoes and garlic on the hot griddle pan for 3–4 minutes, turning occasionally, until they start to soften and char. Remove from the pan and coarsely chop. Put them into a bowl and mix with the other ingredients. Season to taste with salt and pepper.

Lay the slices of halloumi on the hot griddle pan and cook, in batches, for 2–3 minutes on each side, or until crisp, golden brown, and striped.

Place 2 slices of halloumi on each serving plate and cover each one with a slice of eggplant. Top with a spoonful of the griddled tomato salsa and drizzle with balsamic vinegar. Serve immediately while the halloumi is appetizingly hot.

Dips

Tzatziki

Makes 2½ cups (600 ml / 1 pint)
Preparation time 7¼ hours (including draining and chilling)

- 3 cups (750 ml / 1¼ pints) **plain yogurt**
- 1 long, thin **cucumber**, peeled and finely chopped
- 3–4 **garlic cloves**, finely chopped
- ¼ teaspoon **salt**
- 3–4 tablespoons **olive oil**
- 3 tablespoons finely chopped **fresh dill**

Line a strainer with cheesecloth (muslin) or a double thickness of paper towels and spoon the yogurt into it. Let drain over a bowl in the refrigerator for about 6 hours.

Transfer the strained yogurt from the strainer to a bowl. Stir in the cucumber, garlic, salt, and oil. Cover and chill.

Serve in a shallow bowl, sprinkled with the dill. This is excellent with bread, crackers, vegetable fritters, meatballs, or crudités.

Eggplant Dip

Makes 2 cups (450 ml / 16 fl oz)
Preparation time 2 hours (including chilling)
Cooking time 30 minutes

2¼ lb (1 kg) **eggplants** (aubergines)

¼ teaspoon **salt**, plus extra for sprinkling

2–3 **garlic cloves**, finely chopped

½ cup (120 ml / 4 fl oz) **olive oil**, plus extra for sprinkling

about 4 tablespoons **red wine vinegar**

2 tablespoons chopped **fresh parsley**

1 mild **green bell pepper**, seeded and chopped

1 **tomato**, seeded and chopped

Preheat the broiler (grill) or light the barbecue. Broil or grill the eggplants (aubergines), turning frequently, until the skins are charred and the flesh is softened. (Cooking over charcoal gives the salad a pleasant smoky flavor.) Remove from the heat and hold each eggplant briefly under cold running water until cool enough to handle, then peel immediately. Do not allow the unpeeled eggplants to cool completely or the flesh will turn black. When peeled, put them into a strainer and let cool completely.

Chop the eggplant flesh and transfer to a bowl. Add the salt and garlic. Beating constantly with an electric mixer on medium speed, gradually add the oil, a few drops at a time, then in a slow, steady thin stream until all of it has been absorbed. Continue beating and gradually add vinegar to taste, a little at a time.

Transfer to a serving dish, cover, and chill in the refrigerator. Garnish the eggplant dip with the parsley, chopped bell pepper, and tomato. Sprinkle with a little salt and olive oil and serve with crackers or crudités.

Note: You can substitute 2 tablespoons grated onion for the garlic and lemon juice for the vinegar. Alternatively, add ½ cup (120 ml / 4 fl oz) mayonnaise to the eggplant and garlic purée, plus a few drops of Tabasco sauce, if you like.

Garlic Sauce

Makes 2 cups (450 ml / 16 fl oz)
Preparation time 40 minutes

5–6 **garlic cloves**, finely chopped

¾ teaspoon **salt**

2 **potatoes**, about 7 oz (200 g) total weight, cooked and peeled

¾ cup (50 g / 2 oz) day-old **bread crumbs**

4 tablespoons **red wine vinegar**

½ cup (120 ml / 4 fl oz) **olive oil**

Process all the ingredients with 5 tablespoons water in a food processor at medium speed for 1–2 minutes, until smooth and thoroughly mixed. If the sauce is too thick, add some more water and process for 1–2 seconds more, or until the required consistency is reached.

Olive Paste

Makes 1 cup (250 ml / 8 fl oz)
Preparation time 20 minutes

½ cup (50 g / 2 oz) **cashew nuts**

3½ cups (400 g / 14 oz) pitted (stoned) **black olives**, sliced

3 tablespoons **olive oil** (optional)

1–2 tablespoons **red wine vinegar**

½ teaspoon **dried oregano**

1 small **garlic clove** (optional)

Put the nuts into a food processor and grind to a smooth paste. Add the remaining ingredients and process for 1–2 minutes, until the mixture is well blended. Serve with crackers, spread on sandwiches, or use as a sauce for cooked pasta. This is a delicious meze with ouzo.

Taramosalata

Makes 2 cups (450 ml / 16 fl oz)
Preparation time 45 minutes (including chilling)

6 thick slices of day-old **bread**, crusts removed

7 oz (200 g) cured **cod's roe**

2 tablespoons finely chopped **onion**

1¼ cups (300 ml / ½ pint) **olive** or **corn oil**

5 tablespoons freshly squeezed **lemon juice**

3 **scallions** (spring onions), thinly chopped, to garnish

small **Kalamata olives**, to garnish

crispbread, **crackers**, and **ouzo**, to serve

Tear the bread into pieces, put it into a bowl, pour in a little water, and let soak for 5 minutes, then gently squeeze out.

Put the roe, onion, and a third of the oil in a food processor and process for a few seconds, until the roe is broken down and the mixture is blended. Add the soaked bread, a little at a time, processing after each addition until thoroughly blended. With the motor running, gradually add the remaining oil in a thin steady stream through the feeder tube until the mixture is smooth and combined. Add the lemon juice, a little at a time, and process for a few seconds until the paste is thickened and pale pink. If the taramosalata is too thick, add a little club soda (soda water) or water and beat until light and soft.

Transfer to a serving dish, cover, and chill in the refrigerator. Garnish with the scallions (spring onions) and black olives. Serve with crispbread, crackers, and ouzo with ice.

Note: You can substitute 7 oz (200 g) cooked, peeled potatoes for the bread and add ⅔ cup (65 g / 2½ oz) ground unsalted almonds, peanuts, or hazelnuts.

Vefa's secret: Both pink and white fish roe are available. The white is more expensive and delicate in flavor, but the pink gives the taramosalata its lovely color. Using half pink and half white fish roe is, perhaps, the ideal combination. Also, for a lighter texture, use half olive oil and half corn oil.

Soups & Salads

Traditional Easter Soup

Serves 6
Preparation time 30 minutes
Cooking time 65 minutes

1 lb 2 oz (500 g) **lamb's intestines**

red wine vinegar, for sprinkling

salt and **pepper**

1 **lamb's pluck** (liver, heart, and spleen)

½ cup (120 ml / 4 fl oz) **olive oil**

1 cup (80 g / 3 oz) finely chopped **scallions** (spring onions)

1 **onion**, finely chopped

2 cups (450 ml / 16 fl oz) **hot water**

½ cup (25 g / 1 oz) finely chopped **fresh parsley**

½ cup (15 g / ½ oz) finely chopped **fresh dill**

3 tablespoons **tomato paste** (purée)

Wash the intestines well. They are easier to clean if you cut them into 1–3 foot (30–60 cm) lengths and then, with the help of a knitting needle or thin skewer, turn the pieces inside out, and rinse them under cold running water. Put them into a bowl, sprinkle with a little vinegar, and set aside for 10 minutes, then rinse, and drain.

Blanch them in salted water for 5 minutes, drain well, and chop finely.

Blanch the lamb's pluck, drain well, and chop finely.

Heat the oil in a large pan. Add the scallions (spring onions) and onion and cook over low heat, stirring occasionally, for about 5 minutes, until softened and translucent. Add all the chopped meat and cook, stirring constantly, for 5 minutes. Pour in the hot water, cover, and simmer for about 30 minutes, until the meat is almost tender. Add the herbs, stir in the tomato paste (purée), season with salt and pepper, and simmer for 20 minutes more, until the meat is cooked and the liquid has thickened. Serve hot.

Summer Vegetable Soup

Serves 4
Preparation time 15 minutes
Cooking time 25 minutes

5 tablespoons **olive oil**

1 **onion**, coarsely chopped

4 cups (1 litre / 1¾ pints) **chicken** or **vegetable stock**

salt and **pepper**

1½ cups (200 g / 7 oz) **green (French) beans**, cut into short lengths

4 **artichoke hearts**, cut into small pieces

2 **zucchini** (courgettes), diced

¾ cup (80 g / 3 oz) shelled **fresh** or **frozen peas**

10 **white mushrooms**, sliced

4 tablespoons chopped **fresh parsley**

2 **tomatoes**, peeled, seeded, and chopped

3½ oz (100 g) **egg noodles** (pasta)

sesame bread sticks and **feta cheese**, to serve

Heat the oil in a large pan. Add the onion and cook over high heat for 2–3 minutes, until softened and translucent. Pour in the stock and bring to a boil. Season with salt and pepper and add all the remaining ingredients except the noodles. Cover and simmer for about 15 minutes, until all the vegetables are almost tender.

Add the noodles and cook for 8 minutes more, or until al dente.

Serve the soup hot or at room temperature, sprinkled with freshly ground pepper and accompanied by sesame bread sticks and feta cheese.

Greek Fisherman's Soup

Serves 6
Preparation time 1 hour
Cooking time 3 hours 20 minutes

2¼ lb (1 kg) assorted **small fish**, scaled and cleaned

9 oz (250 g) **onions**, thinly sliced

9 oz (250 g) **tomatoes**, peeled and thinly sliced

2–3 tablespoons finely chopped **fresh parsley**

5 tablespoons **olive oil**

salt and **pepper**

Put the fish in a large pan and pour in water to cover. Bring to a boil, cover with a lid, and simmer for 20 minutes.

Remove the fish and discard any large bones.

Strain the stock and return to the pan. Add the fish, onions, tomatoes, parsley, and oil and season with salt and pepper. Cover and simmer over low heat for 2–3 hours, or until the soup is rich and thickened.

Serve hot, sprinkled with freshly ground pepper.

Note: This ancient soup is believed to be a forerunner of *bouillabaisse*. Traditional *kakavia* (Greek Fisherman's Soup) is made by Greek fishermen in a small pot or *kakavi* on the deck of their caique. The pot is lined with onions, then tomatoes and parsley. It is then covered with fish, and simple seasonings, olive oil, and hot water are added. The soup is simmered until the vegetables and fish bones have disintegrated. It is eaten without being strained, accompanied by lots of bread and retsina.

Beet Salad with Garlic Yogurt

Serves 6
Preparation time 5½ hours (including marinating and chilling)
Cooking time 30 minutes

2¼ lb (1 kg) tender young **beets** (beetroots), trimmed

4 tablespoons **red wine vinegar**

4 tablespoons **olive oil**

salt

1 cup (250 ml / 8 fl oz) strained plain or thick **Greek yogurt**

3 **garlic cloves**, finely chopped

⅓ cup (40 g / 1½ oz) coarsely chopped **walnuts**

Put the beets (beetroots) into a pan, add boiling water to cover, and cook for about 30 minutes, or until tender. Rub or peel off the skin and cut into slices. Put the slices on a deep platter and pour half the vinegar and half the olive oil over them. Season with salt, cover, and let marinate at room temperature for 2–3 hours.

Combine the yogurt, the remaining oil, the remaining vinegar, and the garlic in a bowl and season lightly with salt. Pour the mixture over the beet slices, cover, and chill in the refrigerator for 2 hours to let the flavors blend.

Just before serving, sprinkle with the chopped walnuts.

Greek Village Salad

Serves 4
Preparation time 15 minutes

2 large **tomatoes**

1 **cucumber**, peeled and sliced

1 **red onion**, thinly sliced into rings

10 **Kalamata olives**

4 oz (120 g) **feta cheese**, diced

pinch of **dried oregano**

Oil-vinegar dressing (p 20)

2 **hard-boiled eggs**, sliced or quartered (optional)

chopped **fresh parsley**, **watercress**, or **arugula** (rocket), to garnish (optional)

Cut each tomato into 6 wedges.

Combine the tomatoes, cucumber, onion rings, olives, and feta in a large bowl. Sprinkle the salad with a little oregano and pour the oil-vinegar dressing to taste over it. Toss and serve garnished with the eggs, parsley, watercress, or arugula (rocket), if using.

Broiled Zucchini, Halloumi, and Lettuce Salad

Serves 4
Preparation time 10 minutes
Cooking time 10 minutes

9 oz (250 g) small **zucchini** (courgettes)

salt and **pepper**

olive oil, for brushing

9 oz (250 g) **romaine (cos) lettuce hearts**

9 oz (250 g) **radicchio hearts**

5 oz (150 g) **halloumi** or **Provolone cheese**, diced

fresh mint leaves, to garnish

FOR THE DRESSING

3 tablespoons **olive oil**

2 tablespoons **balsamic vinegar**

1 teaspoon **honey**

1 teaspoon **Dijon mustard**

salt and **pepper**

Preheat the broiler (grill). Put all the dressing ingredients into a screw-top jar, season with salt and pepper, fasten the lid, and set aside.

Halve the zucchini (courgettes) lengthwise, season with salt and pepper, and brush with olive oil. Broil (grill) for about 8 minutes, turning once, until tender and lightly browned. Remove from the broiler and cut them diagonally into bite-size pieces. Put them into a bowl.

Shake the jar of dressing vigorously until thoroughly combined, then pour it over the zucchini.

Just before serving, tear the lettuce and radicchio into pieces and place them in a deep salad bowl. Pour the dressed zucchini over them. Put the cheese on a sheet of aluminum foil and broil until lightly browned. Sprinkle the pieces of cheese over the salad, garnish with mint leaves, and serve immediately.

Potato Salad with Octopus

Serves 6
Preparation time 2½ hours (including marinating)
Cooking time 20–25 minutes

1 lb 2 oz (500 g) small **octopuses**, cleaned (p 104)

1 lb 2 oz (500 g) **potatoes**

salt

1 large ripe **avocado**

2 tablespoons freshly squeezed **lemon** or **lime juice**

1 bunch **arugula** (rocket), trimmed

2 **scallions** (spring onions), thinly sliced

toasted **garlic bread** or **croutons**, to serve

FOR THE MARINADE

2 tablespoons **olive oil**

4 tablespoons freshly squeezed **lemon** or **lime juice**

1 **red chile**, finely chopped

1 **garlic clove**, finely chopped

FOR THE TOMATO DRESSING

4 small **tomatoes**, peeled and cubed

4 tablespoons finely chopped **fresh parsley**

1 small **onion**, finely chopped

2 tablespoons **red wine vinegar**

3 tablespoons **olive oil**

1 tablespoon **balsamic vinegar**

pepper

Rinse the octopuses, cut in half (unless they are very small), and put into a bowl.

Put all the ingredients for the marinade in a screw-top jar, fasten the lid, and shake vigorously until thoroughly blended. Pour the mixture over the octopuses and let marinate in the refrigerator for at least 2 hours.

Cook the potatoes in salted boiling water for 15–20 minutes, until tender. (You could also cook them in the microwave if you like.) Drain and let cool, then cut into bite-size pieces.

Combine all the dressing ingredients in a bowl and season with pepper.

Preheat the broiler (grill). Meanwhile, peel the avocado, cut it in half lengthwise, and remove the pit (stone). Dice the flesh and toss with the lemon or lime juice in a bowl to prevent discoloration.

Drain the octopuses and broil (grill), turning once or twice, for about 5 minutes, until the tentacles are twisted.

Arrange the arugula (rocket) leaves on a platter. Spoon the potatoes over them and sprinkle with the avocado and scallions (spring onions). Arrange the octopuses on top and sprinkle the salad with the dressing.

Serve immediately, accompanied by toasted garlic bread or croutons.

Vegetables

Artichokes and Fava Beans

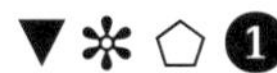

Serves 4
Preparation time 1 hour
Cooking time 30 minutes

2¼ lb (1 kg) young **fava (broad) beans** in their pods, trimmed

5 **globe artichokes**

3 tablespoons freshly squeezed **lemon juice**

½ cup (120 ml / 4 fl oz) **olive oil**

1 cup (100 g / 3½ oz) finely chopped **scallions** (spring onions)

½ cup (15 g / ½ oz) finely chopped **fresh dill**

salt and **pepper**

lemon wedges, to garnish

feta cheese, to serve

Cut the tender fava (broad) bean pods in half and shell the larger beans. Break off the stems of the artichokes, cut the bases flat, and pull off any small base leaves. Remove any tough outer leaves and scoop out the hairy choke from the center, leaving only the cup-shaped heart. As you prepare each artichoke, put it into a bowl of water with 1 tablespoon of the lemon juice to prevent discoloration.

Heat the oil in a pan over medium heat. Add the scallions (spring onions) and cook over low heat, stirring occasionally, for about 5 minutes, until softened. Add the beans, drained artichokes, and dill, season with salt and pepper, and pour in 1 cup (250 ml / 8 fl oz) water. Cover and simmer for about 30 minutes, or until the beans and artichokes are tender and the sauce has reduced.

Remove from the heat and sprinkle the vegetables with the remaining lemon juice, gently shaking the pan to distribute it evenly.

Serve hot or at room temperature, garnished with lemon wedges and accompanied by feta cheese.

Fricasee of Oyster Mushrooms

Serves 4
Preparation time 15 minutes
Cooking time 40 minutes

1 lb 2 oz (500 g) **scallions** (spring onions), cut into short lengths

5 tablespoons **olive oil**

1 lb 2 oz (500 g) **oyster mushrooms**, cut into large pieces

9 oz (250 g) **romaine (cos) lettuce**, cut into pieces

4 tablespoons finely chopped **fresh dill**

½ cup (25 g / 1 oz) finely chopped **fresh parsley**

salt and **pepper**

½ cup (120 ml / 4 fl oz) **hot water**

1 **egg**

4 tablespoons freshly squeezed **lemon juice**

Briefly blanch the scallions (spring onions) in boiling water, then drain.

Heat the oil in a large pan. Add the mushrooms and cook over low heat, stirring occasionally, for 8–10 minutes, until softened. Add the scallions, lettuce, dill, and parsley, season with salt and pepper, and pour in the hot water. Bring to a boil, cover, and simmer for 30 minutes, until the vegetables are tender but still firm and the liquid has reduced to a thick sauce.

Beat the egg with the lemon juice in a bowl and whisk in a ladleful of the pan juices, then pour the egg-lemon mixture into the pan, shaking it gently to distribute it evenly. Serve hot.

Vefa's secret: This vegetarian dish will also appeal to carnivores. To make it for vegans, omit the egg and finish the dish only with lemon juice. Without egg-lemon sauce, it is also good served at room temperature.

Stuffed Vegetables

Serves 6
Preparation time 45 minutes
Cooking time 2¼ hours

3 large **tomatoes**
1 **green bell pepper**
1 **red bell pepper**
1 **yellow bell pepper**
2 small round **zucchini** (courgettes)
1 large round **eggplant** (aubergine)
¾ cup (175 ml / 6 fl oz) **olive oil**
1 large **onion**, grated
2¼ cups (450 g / 1 lb) **medium-grain rice**
½ cup (25 g / 1 oz) finely chopped **fresh mint**
3 tablespoons **tomato paste** (purée)
1 tablespoon **tomato ketchup**
¼ teaspoon **ground allspice**
2 large **potatoes**, cut into wedges
1 cup (250 ml / 8 fl oz) **tomato juice**
salt and **pepper**

Slice off and reserve the tops of the tomatoes, bell peppers, and zucchini (courgettes). Scoop out the pulp from the tomatoes and zucchini with a spoon and seed the bell peppers without piercing the skin. Sprinkle the interior of the vegetable "shells" with a little salt and set aside. Cut the eggplant (aubergine) in half lengthwise and scoop out most of the flesh to form 2 shells.

Blanch the eggplant and zucchini shells in boiling water for 5 minutes, then drain. Arrange all the vegetable shells in a large ovenproof dish.

Finely chop the scooped-out flesh from the tomatoes, eggplant, and zucchini.

Heat half the oil in a pan over high heat. Add the onion and cook, stirring frequently, for 3–4 minutes, until softened. Add the tomato, eggplant, and zucchini flesh and cook over high heat, stirring frequently, for 10 minutes.

Remove from the heat, stir in the rice, mint, tomato paste (purée), tomato ketchup, and allspice, and season with salt and pepper.

Preheat the oven to 350°F (180°C / Gas Mark 4).

Fill the vegetable shells three-quarters full with the mixture and replace the tops on the tomatoes, bell peppers, and zucchini. (If there is any filling left over, use it to stuff zucchini flowers.) Put the potato wedges between the stuffed vegetables, pour the tomato juice on top, and sprinkle with a little salt and pepper. Spoon the remaining olive oil over the potatoes and the stuffed vegetables. Bake for about 2 hours, or until lightly browned. If the tops begin to brown too quickly, cover loosely with a piece of aluminum foil. It may be necessary to add some water during baking to prevent sticking. Serve hot or at room temperature.

Mixed Spring Vegetable Stew

Serves 4
Preparation time 1 hour
Cooking time 45 minutes

4 **globe artichokes**

1 **lemon**, halved

1 tablespoon **all-purpose (plain) flour**

1 tablespoon freshly squeezed **lemon juice**

⅔ cup (150 ml / ¼ pint) **olive oil**

1 **onion**, grated

2¼ lb (1 kg) ripe **tomatoes**, peeled, seeded, and finely chopped or 14 oz (400 g) canned chopped tomatoes

1 teaspoon **sugar**

1 tablespoon **red wine vinegar**

½ cup (25 g / 1 oz) finely chopped **fresh parsley** or (15 g / ½ oz) **dill**

salt and **pepper**

1 lb 2 oz (500 g) young **fava (broad) beans** in their pods, trimmed and halved

2¼ lb (1 kg) **potatoes**, quartered

2¼ lb (1 kg) **fresh peas**, shelled

Cut off the artichoke stems, trim the bases, and remove all the thick green leaves and the chokes, leaving only the cup-shaped hearts. Rub with the lemon halves to prevent discoloration and place in a bowl of water mixed with the flour and lemon juice.

Heat the oil in a large pan. Add the onion and cook over low heat, stirring occasionally, for 5 minutes, until softened. Add the tomatoes, sugar, vinegar, and parsley or dill and season with salt and pepper. Add the beans, drained artichoke hearts, potatoes, and peas, cover, and simmer for about 40 minutes, until the vegetables are tender and the sauce has reduced.

Serve the vegetable stew (*tourlou*) hot or at room temperature. This recipe can be easily adapted to suit whatever vegetables you have on hand.

Legumes & Pasta

Bean, Spinach, and Sausage Casserole

Serves 4
Preparation time 24½ hours (including soaking)
Cooking time 1½ hours

11 oz (300 g) dried **giant white beans** or **lima (butter) beans**, soaked for 24 hours in cold water to cover and drained

½ cup (120 ml / 4 fl oz) **olive oil**

9 oz (250 g) **pork sausages**, cut into bite-size pieces

1 **onion**, grated

2 **garlic cloves**, finely chopped

1 lb 2 oz (500 g) ripe **tomatoes**, peeled and finely chopped or 14 oz (400 g) canned chopped tomatoes

4 tablespoons finely chopped **fresh parsley**

salt and **pepper**

1 lb 2 oz (500 g) fresh **spinach**, rinsed and coarse stalks removed

Put the beans into a pan, pour in water to cover, and bring to a boil. Reduce the heat and simmer for about 30 minutes, then drain, and tip into an ovenproof dish.

Preheat the oven to 350°F (180°C / Gas Mark 4). Meanwhile, heat half the oil in a skillet or frying pan. Add the sausage, onion, and garlic and cook over low heat for 5 minutes, until the onion has softened. Stir in the tomatoes and parsley, season with salt and pepper, and simmer for 5 minutes.

Pour the mixture over the beans, stir well, and bake, adding a little hot water if necessary, for about 50 minutes, until the beans are soft.

Meanwhile, roughly chop the spinach, and cook over low heat for 2–3 minutes, until wilted. Drain well.

Heat the remaining olive oil in a skillet or frying pan, add the spinach, and cook over low heat for about 5 minutes. Remove the beans from the oven and dot with the spinach. Bake for 5 minutes more. Serve hot.

Garbanzo Bean and Eggplant Casserole

Serves 4
Preparation time 13½ hours (including soaking)
Cooking time 2½ hours

1⅓ cups (300 g / 11 oz) **dried garbanzo beans** (chickpeas), soaked for 12 hours in cold water to cover with 1 tablespoon salt

¾ cup (175 ml / 6 fl oz) **olive oil**, plus extra for drizzling

1 large **onion**, sliced

4 **garlic cloves**, thinly sliced

14 oz (400 g) canned **chopped tomatoes**

½ teaspoon **ground allspice**

1 teaspoon **paprika**

½ teaspoon **dried oregano**, plus extra for sprinkling

salt and **pepper**

4 large **eggplants** (aubergines), cut in ¼-inch (5-mm) thick slices

3 large **tomatoes**, thinly sliced

Drain and rinse the garbanzo beans (chickpeas) and put them into a large pan with water to cover. Bring to a boil, skimming off the scum that rises to the surface, cover, and simmer for 30 minutes.

Heat 4 tablespoons of the oil in a small skillet or frying pan. Add the onion and garlic and cook over low heat, stirring occasionally, for 5 minutes, until softened.

Add the contents of the skillet to the garbanzo beans with the canned tomatoes, allspice, paprika, and oregano. Season with salt and pepper and simmer for 1 hour more, until the garbanzo beans are tender.

Meanwhile, sprinkle the eggplant slices with salt and let drain in a colander for 1 hour. Rinse, drain, and squeeze out the excess moisture.

Preheat the oven to 350°F (180°C / Gas Mark 4).

Heat the remaining oil in a skillet or frying pan. Add the eggplant slices and cook, turning frequently, for about 8 minutes. Remove with a slotted spoon and drain.

Arrange half the eggplant slices on the base of an ovenproof dish. Spread the garbanzo bean mixture over them and cover with the remaining eggplant slices. Top with the tomato slices, sprinkle with oregano, season with salt and pepper, and drizzle with a little olive oil. Bake for about 50 minutes.

Serve hot or at room temperature.

Lentils with Rice and Onions

Serves 4
Preparation time 10 minutes
Cooking time 35 minutes

1⅓ cups (300 g / 11 oz) **green lentils**

4 cups (1 litre / 1¾ pints) **boiling water**

½ cup (100 g / 3½ oz) **long-grain rice**

2 tablespoons freshly squeezed **lemon juice**

salt and **pepper**

½ cup (120 ml / 4 fl oz) **olive oil**

3 **onions**, sliced

olives and **Taramosalata** (p 47), to serve

Put the lentils into a pan, pour in water to cover, bring to a boil, and cook for 5 minutes over high heat. Drain well, return to the pan, and pour in the boiling water, then cover and cook for 10 minutes.

Add the rice and lemon juice, season with salt and pepper, re-cover the pan, and simmer for 20 minutes more, until the lentils and rice are tender and all the liquid has been absorbed.

Meanwhile, heat the oil in a skillet or frying pan. Add the onions and cook over low heat, stirring occasionally, for 8–10 minutes, until lightly browned.

Stir the onions into the lentil and rice mixture. Serve hot, accompanied by olives and Taramosalata.

Rice with Shellfish and Tomato Sauce

Serves 6
Preparation time 20 minutes
Cooking time 45 minutes

1 lb 2 oz (500 g) raw **shrimp** (prawns)

1 tablespoon **paprika**

1 lb 2 oz (500 g) raw **shelled mussels**

2 cups (400 g / 14 oz) **basmati rice**

FOR THE SAUCE

1 large **onion**, sliced

2 **leeks**, white part only, finely chopped

3 **garlic cloves**, finely chopped

½ **green bell pepper**, seeded and cut into julienne strips

½ **red bell pepper**, seeded and cut into julienne strips

4 ripe **tomatoes**, peeled, seeded, and chopped

1 teaspoon **sugar**

1 tablespoon **red wine vinegar**

4 tablespoons finely chopped **fresh dill** or **parsley**

½ teaspoon **cayenne pepper**

salt and **pepper**

Peel and devein the shrimp (prawns), following the instructions on page 102, leaving the heads intact.

Bring 3 cups (750 ml / 1¼ pints) water to a boil in pan. Stir in the paprika, add the shrimp and mussels, and cook for 5 minutes. Using a slotted spoon, transfer to a bowl. Remove and discard the heads of the shrimp and cut the shrimp into pieces.

Strain the cooking liquid through a cheesecloth- (muslin-) lined strainer into a bowl, measure, and make up to 3 cups (750 ml /1¼ pints) with water. Pour into a pan and bring to a boil. Add the rice and simmer for about 20 minutes, until all the liquid has been absorbed and the rice is fluffy.

Meanwhile, prepare the sauce. Cook the onion, leeks, garlic, and bell peppers in a pan with 1 tablespoon water until softened. Add the tomatoes, sugar, vinegar, dill, and cayenne pepper and simmer until slightly thickened.

Remove from the heat, add the cooked shrimp and mussels, and season with salt and pepper. Spoon the rice onto a platter and pour the shellfish and tomato mixture on top.

Cheese-filled Pasta

Serves 10–12
Preparation time 14 hours (including resting and drying)
Cooking time 10 minutes

4½ cups (500 g / 1 lb 2 oz) **all-purpose (plain) flour**, plus extra for dusting

1 teaspoon **salt**

2 **eggs**, lightly beaten

melted **butter**, to serve

FOR THE FILLING

11 oz (300 g) **anthotiro** or **ricotta cheese**

¼ teaspoon **ground allspice** or freshly grated **nutmeg**

½ teaspoon **saffron threads**, crumbled

pepper

To make the dough, sift together the flour and salt into a bowl. Mix in the eggs and knead, adding enough water to make a firm, elastic dough (2–3 tablespoons). Let rest for 1 hour.

Meanwhile, prepare the filling. Combine all the filling ingredients in a bowl and season with pepper.

Divide the dough into 6–8 pieces and roll out on a lightly floured work surface into very thin sheets. Cut into strips 2½ × 3 inches (6 × 8 cm). Place a teaspoon of filling along the center of each strip, roll up from the long side, and twist the ends together, sealing them with your fingers. They will resemble tiny Christmas crackers. Arrange the parcels (*latzania*) on a floured dish towel and let dry for up to 12 hours.

Cook in plenty of salted boiling water for about 8–10 minutes, or until tender. Remove with a slotted spoon and serve hot, drizzled with sizzling melted butter.

Feta Omelet with Egg Noodles

Serves 4
Preparation time 10 minutes
Cooking time 20 minutes

5 oz (150 g) **long egg noodles** (pasta), such as tagliatelle

6 **eggs**

9 oz (250 g) **feta cheese**, crumbled

⅓ cup (80 g / 3 oz) melted **clarified butter**

pepper

Cook the noodles (pasta) in salted boiling water for 10 minutes, or until just tender, then drain and tip into a bowl.

Lightly beat the eggs in another bowl and stir in the crumbled feta. Fold the cheese mixture into the noodles.

Heat half the butter in a large deep skillet or frying pan, add the noodles, and cook until crisp. Invert onto a large plate. Add the remaining butter to the skillet and heat. Slide the noodle omelet into the skillet and cook the second side until crisp.

Remove from the heat, season with pepper, cut into wedges, and serve immediately.

Orzo with Vegetables

Serves 4
Preparation time 1½ hours (including salting)
Cooking time 1 hour

- 2 **eggplants** (aubergines), diced
- 2 **zucchini** (courgettes), cut in half lengthwise and sliced
- **salt** and **pepper**
- ½ cup (120 ml / 4 fl oz) **olive oil**
- 1 **onion**, grated
- 2 **garlic cloves**, finely chopped
- 12 oz (350 g) **orzo pasta**
- 1 **celery stalk**, thinly sliced
- 2 **carrots**, thinly sliced
- 2¼ lb (1 kg) **tomatoes**, peeled, seeded, and chopped
- 2 cups (450 ml / 16 fl oz) **hot water**
- ½ cup (50 g / 2 oz) **grated kefalotiri** or **Parmesan cheese**

Sprinkle the eggplants (aubergines) and zucchini (courgettes) with salt and let drain in separate colanders for 1 hour. Rinse and squeeze out the excess water.

Preheat the oven to 350°F (180°C / Gas Mark 4).

Heat half the olive oil in a large pan over high heat. Add the onion and garlic and cook, stirring frequently, for 3–4 minutes, until softened. Add the eggplants and zucchini, reduce the heat to medium, and cook, stirring occasionally, for about 8 minutes, until lightly browned.

Heat the remaining oil in another pan. Add the pasta and cook over medium heat, stirring constantly, for 2–3 minutes. Transfer to an ovenproof dish, add the zucchini, eggplants, celery, and carrots, and season with salt and pepper. Add the tomatoes and pour in the hot water. Bake, adding more hot water if necessary, for 1 hour, until the pasta is tender.

Serve hot, sprinkled with the grated cheese.

Note: For a better texture, you can also fry the eggplants and zucchini in hot oil, drain on paper towels, and add to the dish 15 minutes before the end of the cooking time.

Stuffed Pasta

Serves 6
Preparation time 1½ hours (including resting)
Cooking time 15 minutes

4½ cups (500 g / 1 lb 2 oz) **all-purpose (plain) flour**, plus extra for dusting (optional)

1 teaspoon **salt**

2 **eggs**, lightly beaten

1 cup (250 g / 8 oz) **butter**

8¾ cups (2 liters / 3½ pints) **beef stock**

1 cup (250 ml / 8 fl oz) **sheep's milk yogurt**

1 **garlic clove**, crushed

FOR THE FILLING

1 lb 2 oz (500 g) **ground (minced) beef**

1 large **onion**, grated

2 tablespoons finely chopped **fresh parsley** (optional)

salt and **pepper**

To make the dough, sift together the flour and salt into a bowl, make a well in the center, and add the beaten eggs. Gradually mix in the dry ingredients, adding a little water at a time—no more than ½ cup (120 ml / 4 fl oz)—to make a smooth, firm dough that comes away from your fingers. Shape it into a ball, cover with plastic wrap (cling film), and let rest for 30 minutes.

To make the filling, combine the ground (minced) meat, onion, and parsley in a bowl and season with salt and pepper.

Using a pasta machine, roll out strips of dough very thinly. Alternatively, roll out by hand on a lightly floured work surface. Cut the strips into 1-inch (2.5-cm) squares. Place a small piece of filling, about the size of a hazelnut, in the center of each square. Moisten the edges with water and fold the opposite corners of the squares over the filling and press to seal them.

Melt half the butter in a heavy skillet or frying pan and fry the *manti* (see Note), until golden.

Bring the stock to a boil in a pan, add the *manti*, and cook for 15 minutes, until tender.

Meanwhile, melt the remaining butter in a small pan. Drain the *manti*, transfer to a deep platter, and pour the melted butter over them. Whisk together the yogurt and garlic in a bowl. Serve the pasta immediately with the garlic yogurt.

Alternatively, you could place the *manti* in a greased ovenproof dish, pour the melted butter over the top, and bake in an oven preheated to 350°F (180°C / Gas Mark 4), until lightly browned. Pour the stock over them and cover with aluminum foil. Reduce the heat to 300°F (150°C / Gas Mark 2) and bake, adding more stock if necessary, until tender.

Note: The *manti* of Asia Minor is a dish consisting of tiny pieces of pasta dough filled with meat or other fillings.

Fish & Shellfish

Gilt-head Sea Bream Baked in Parcels

Serves 4
Preparation time 45 minutes (including chilling)
Cooking time 45 minutes

2 **gilt-head sea bream** or **porgy**, about 1 lb 10 oz (750 g) each, scaled, cleaned, and filleted

salt and **pepper**

generous ½ cup (135 ml / 4½ fl oz) **olive oil**, plus extra for brushing

2 **potatoes**, sliced into rounds

1 small **fennel bulb**, sliced

1 **carrot**, sliced

1 **celery stalk** with leaves, chopped

1 **zucchini** (courgette), sliced

1 cup (250 ml / 8 fl oz) **dry white wine**

2 tablespoons finely chopped **fresh dill**

1 large **tomato**, sliced into rounds

4 fresh **rosemary sprigs**

Remove any pin bones from the fish with tweezers, season with salt and pepper, brush with oil, and chill for 30 minutes.

Meanwhile, cook the potatoes in a pan of salted boiling water for 10 minutes.

Heat 2½ tablespoons of the oil in a pan. Add the fennel, carrot, celery, and zucchini (courgette) and cook over high heat, stirring frequently, for 5 minutes. Pour in half the wine and let the alcohol evaporate, then cover and simmer for 10 minutes, or until the vegetables are almost tender. Add the dill, season with salt and pepper, and remove from the heat.

Heat 2½ tablespoons of the remaining oil in a nonstick skillet or frying pan. Cook the fish fillets, skin side down, in batches for a few minutes until lightly browned.

Preheat the oven to 400°F (200°C / Gas Mark 6).

Cut 4 pieces of wax (greaseproof) paper into 12 × 16-inch (30 × 40-cm) rectangles. Make a bed of potato slices in the center of each rectangle. Spread one quarter of the vegetables on top of the potatoes and top with the fish, skin side down. Place a tomato slice and a rosemary sprig on each fish. Sprinkle 1 tablespoon each of olive oil and wine over each, and season with salt and pepper. Fold the sides over the fish and twist the edges to seal. Place in a roasting pan and bake for 15 minutes. Serve in the parcels.

Fish Stew

Serves 6
Preparation time 1¼ hours (including marinating)
Cooking time 40 minutes

3¼ lb (1.5 kg) **mixed fish**, such as scorpion fish, snapper, and perch, scaled and cleaned

freshly squeezed **juice of 1 lemon**

sea salt and **pepper**

1 lb 2 oz (500 g) **onions**, finely chopped

3–4 **garlic cloves**, finely chopped

2 **bay leaves**

1 teaspoon **dried thyme**

1 teaspoon **dried rosemary**

1 cup (250 ml / 8 fl oz) **dry white wine**

1–2 teaspoons **cayenne pepper**

2 tablespoons **tomato paste** (purée) mixed with 4 tablespoons freshly squeezed **lemon juice** (optional)

¾ cup (175 ml / 6 fl oz) **olive oil**

Sprinkle the fish with lemon juice and sea salt and set aside for 1 hour.

Drain and place in a shallow, wide pan. Add the onions, garlic, bay leaves, thyme, rosemary, and wine. Sprinkle with plenty of cayenne and black pepper. Add the tomato paste (purée) mixture, if using, and the oil. Bring to a boil, cover, and simmer for 40 minutes, until the cooking liquid has reduced and the fish flakes easily. Serve immediately.

Red Mullet Baked in Grape Leaves

Serves 4
Preparation time 45 minutes (including chilling)
Cooking time 20 minutes

4 **red mullet** or **snapper**, 2¼ lb (1 kg) total weight, scaled and cleaned

salt and **pepper**

½ cup (120 ml / 4 fl oz) **olive oil**, plus extra for brushing

5 **garlic cloves**, finely chopped

½ cup (25 g / 1 oz) finely chopped **fresh parsley**

5 oz (150 g) **grape (vine) leaves**, blanched

4 tablespoons freshly squeezed **lemon juice**

1 **lemon**, thinly sliced

Rinse the fish under cold running water and pat dry with paper towels. Season with salt and pepper, brush with a little oil, and chill in the refrigerator for 30 minutes.

Preheat the oven to 350°F (180°C / Gas Mark 4) and brush an ovenproof dish with oil.

Combine the garlic and parsley in a bowl, season with salt and pepper, and divide the mixture among the cavities of the fish. Wrap each fish in 1 or 2 grape (vine) leaves, depending on its size, leaving the heads and tails uncovered. Put the fish into the prepared dish, pour the oil and lemon juice over them, and place a slice of lemon on each.

Bake for about 20 minutes, or until the fish flakes easily, and serve immediately.

Cuttlefish with Mixed Greens and Rice

Serves 6
Preparation time 1 hour
Cooking time 1 hour

2¼ lb (1 kg) **cuttlefish**, cleaned (p 14)

2¼ lb (1 kg) **mixed greens**, such as amaranth, nettles, sorrel, and spinach, coarse stalks removed

½ cup (120 ml / 4 fl oz) **olive oil**

1 **onion**, finely chopped

½ cup (50 g / 2 oz) finely chopped **scallions** (spring onions)

4 tablespoons **brandy**

1 cup (250 ml / 8 fl oz) **hot water**

½ cup (15 g / ½ oz) finely chopped **fresh dill**

½ cup (100 g / 3½ oz) **long-grain rice**

salt and **pepper**

4 tablespoons freshly squeezed **lemon juice**

Cut the cuttlefish body sacs into bite-size pieces, but leave the tentacles whole. Put the cuttlefish into a colander and rinse under cold running water, then drain and pat dry.

Put 2 tablespoons water into a large pan and bring to a boil. Add the greens and cook for 5 minutes, then drain, squeezing out as much liquid as possible.

Heat the oil in another large pan. Add the onion and scallions (spring onions) and cook over low heat, stirring occasionally, for 5 minutes, until softened and translucent. Add the cuttlefish, increase the heat to high, and cook, stirring constantly, until their liquid has evaporated. Add the brandy and cook until the alcohol has evaporated. Pour in the hot water, cover, and simmer for 30 minutes, or until the cuttlefish are tender.

Add the greens, dill, and rice, season with salt and pepper, and simmer for 20 minutes more, until the rice and greens are tender.

Mix the lemon juice with a little hot cooking liquid in a bowl, then add to the pan, shaking it to distribute the mixture evenly. Cook for 1 minute more. Serve hot or at room temperature.

Shrimp Casserole with Vegetables

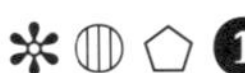

Serves 4
Preparation time 30 minutes
Cooking time 45 minutes

2¼ lb (1 kg) **shrimp** (prawns)

½ cup (120 ml / 4 fl oz) **olive oil**

2 **onions**, sliced

4 **garlic cloves**, thinly sliced

1 large **leek**, white part only, finely chopped

14 oz (400 g) canned **chopped tomatoes**

1 tablespoon **tomato paste** (purée)

2 **celery stalks**, sliced

1 **yellow bell pepper**, seeded and cut into julienne strips

1 **Florina** or other **red bell pepper**, seeded and cut into julienne strips

1 **green bell pepper**, seeded and cut into julienne strips

salt and **pepper**

½ cup (120 ml / 4 fl oz) **hot water**

½ cup (25 g / 1 oz) finely chopped **fresh parsley**

Peel the shrimp (prawns), leaving the heads intact, and devein (make a cut along the back of each shrimp and lift out the vein with a pointed skewer or knife).

Heat the oil in a pan. Add the onions, garlic, and leek and cook over low heat, stirring occasionally, for 5 minutes, until softened. Add the tomatoes, tomato paste (purée), celery, and bell peppers, season with salt and pepper, and pour in the hot water. Bring to a boil, cover, and simmer for about 30 minutes, until the vegetables are tender and the liquid has cooked down to the oil.

Lay the shrimp on top, sprinkle with the parsley, season with salt and pepper, and cook for 8 minutes more. Serve hot.

Note: The word *plaki* usually refers to fish baked in the oven. Here the shrimp are combined with the usual vegetables, but cooked on the stove top (hob) instead.

Octopus with Eggplants

Serves 4
Preparation time 1 hour (including salting)
Cooking time 1 hour 40 minutes

3¼ lb (1.5 kg) **octopus**, cleaned (see Note)

4 tablespoons **red wine vinegar**

1 **bay leaf**

20 **black peppercorns**

4½ lb (2 kg) **eggplants** (aubergines), cut into bite-size pieces

salt and **pepper**

1 cup (250 ml / 8 fl oz) **olive oil**

1 **onion**, grated

1 **garlic clove**, thinly sliced

3 large ripe **tomatoes**, peeled, seeded, and finely chopped

1 teaspoon **sugar**

2 tablespoons **balsamic vinegar**

4 tablespoons finely chopped **fresh parsley**

Put the octopus into a large pan, add the vinegar, bay leaf, and peppercorns, and pour in water to cover. Cook for about 45 minutes.

Meanwhile, sprinkle the eggplants (aubergines) with salt and let drain in a colander for 30 minutes.

Heat half the oil in a pan. Add the onion and garlic and cook over low heat, stirring occasionally, for 5 minutes, until softened. Add the tomatoes, sugar, and balsamic vinegar, season with salt and pepper, and cook for 5 minutes.

Drain the octopus, cut into bite-size pieces, and add to the sauce. Cover and simmer for about 35 minutes, or until the octopus is tender and the sauce has thickened.

Meanwhile, rinse the eggplants, drain, and squeeze out the excess moisture. Heat the remaining oil in a skillet or frying pan. Add the eggplants and cook over medium heat, stirring frequently, for 8–10 minutes, until lightly golden, then remove and drain on paper towels.

Add the eggplants and parsley to the sauce and simmer for 10 minutes more. Serve hot or at room temperature.

Note: To clean an octopus, turn the body inside out and pull out the entrails, including the ink sac. Remove and discard the cartilage-like strips on the sides of the body and the stomach sac. Rinse well, turn the octopus the right way out, and pinch out the beak from the center of the tentacles.

Meat

Chicken with Lemon Sauce and Potatoes

Serves 4
Preparation time 15 minutes
Cooking time 1¼ hours

¾ cup (175 ml / 6 fl oz) **olive oil**

1 **chicken**, about 3¼ lb (1.5 kg), cut into serving pieces

5 tablespoons freshly squeezed **lemon juice**

4½ lb (2 kg) **potatoes**, cut into pieces

pinch of **dried oregano**

salt and **pepper**

Heat the oil in a large pan over high heat. Add the chicken pieces and cook, turning occasionally, for 8–10 minutes, until lightly browned on all sides.

Pour in the lemon juice, add the potatoes and oregano, and season with salt and pepper. Add enough hot water to cover the potatoes, reduce the heat, cover, and simmer for about 1 hour, or until the chicken and potatoes are tender and the sauce has reduced. Serve immediately.

Alternatively, fry the chicken in 4 tablespoons oil and brown the potatoes in the remainder. Add them to the casserole 20 minutes before the end of the cooking time.

Chicken with Olives

Serves 4
Preparation time 15 minutes
Cooking time 1¼ hours

1 **chicken**, about 3¼ lb (1.5 kg), quartered

salt and **pepper**

5 tablespoons **olive oil**

3 **garlic cloves**, thinly sliced

1 tablespoon finely chopped **fresh thyme**, **marjoram**, or **oregano**

5 tablespoons **dry white wine**

1¾ lb (800 g) **tomatoes**, peeled and finely chopped, or 14 oz (400 g) canned **chopped tomatoes**

1¼ cups (150 g / 5 oz) **Kalamata olives**, pitted (stoned) and halved

spaghetti, to serve

Season the chicken with salt and pepper. Heat the oil in a pan. Add the chicken and cook over medium heat, turning occasionally, for 8–10 minutes, until lightly browned all over.

Add the garlic and thyme and cook, stirring constantly, for 5 minutes. Pour in the wine and simmer until the alcohol has evaporated. Add the tomatoes, cover, and simmer for 30 minutes.

Add the olives, re-cover the pan, and simmer for 30 minutes more, until the chicken is tender and the sauce has thickened.

Transfer the chicken to a platter and pour the sauce over it. Serve immediately with spaghetti.

Chicken Souvlaki

⬠

Serves 4
Preparation time 6½ hours (including marinating and soaking)
Cooking time 10–15 minutes

1¾ lb (800 g) skinless, boneless **chicken breast portions**, cut into 1-inch (2.5-cm) cubes

pinch of **dried oregano**, plus extra for sprinkling

2–3 tablespoons **olive oil**

salt and **pepper**

2 **onions**, quartered (optional)

2 **green bell peppers**, seeded and cut into 1-inch (2.5-cm) squares (optional)

1–2 tablespoons freshly squeezed **lemon juice**

Pita bread (p 148), **Tzatziki** (p 42), and lemon wedges, to serve

Put the chicken into a large bowl, add the oregano and oil, season with pepper, and toss well. Cover and let marinate in the refrigerator, turning occasionally, for 6 hours or overnight.

Preheat the broiler (grill) or light the barbecue. If using wooden skewers, soak them in cold water for 30 minutes before using so they don't burn.

Drain and thread the meat onto skewers, alternating with the onions and bell peppers, if using. Drain the oil into a screw-top jar, add the lemon juice, fasten the lid, and shake vigorously until thoroughly combined. Brush the souvlaki with the mixture.

Grill the skewers over charcoal or cook under the broiler, turning twice and brushing frequently with the oil-lemon marinade, for 10–15 minutes, or until the chicken is cooked through. Do not overcook, as chicken is lean and tends to dry out.

Season with salt, sprinkle with oregano, and serve immediately with Pita bread, Tzatziki, and lemon wedges.

Chicken Stew with Okra

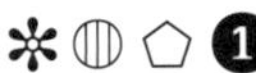

Serves 4
Preparation time 40 minutes
Cooking time 1 hour 30 minutes

7 tablespoons **olive oil**

1 **chicken**, 3¼ lb (1.5 kg), cut into serving pieces

1 small **onion**, grated

1 lb 2 oz (500 g) fresh **tomatoes**, peeled and puréed, or 14 oz (400 g) **canned tomatoes**, puréed

3 tablespoons **red wine vinegar**

1 teaspoon **sugar**

salt and **pepper**

1 lb 2 oz (500 g) **okra**

4 **lemon slices**, rind removed

1 **tomato**, sliced

Heat 5 tablespoons oil in a large pan. Add the chicken and cook over medium heat, turning frequently, for 8–10 minutes, until lightly browned all over. Remove with a slotted spoon and set aside. Add the onion to the pan and cook over low heat, stirring occasionally, for 5 minutes, until softened. Return the chicken to the pan, pour in the tomatoes, add 1 tablespoon vinegar and the sugar, and season with pepper. Cover and simmer for about 1 hour.

Cut the stems off the okra, taking care not to pierce the pods. Dip the cut ends into salt, place in a colander, sprinkle with the remaining vinegar, and set aside for 30 minutes. Rinse under cold running water and drain well.

When the chicken is almost cooked and the sauce is thick, add the okra and lemon slices, shaking the pan to distribute them evenly. Put the tomato slices on top, season with salt and pepper, and sprinkle with the remaining oil. Cover and simmer for about 15 minutes, or until the okra is tender but firm.

Alternatively, you can cook the stew in the oven. Preheat the oven to 350°F (180°C / Gas Mark 4). Cover with aluminum foil and bake for about 45 minutes, or until the chicken is tender. Stir in the okra halfway through the cooking time, and add a little extra water if necessary. Serve immediately, seasoned with pepper.

ZANAE
ΤΟΜΑΤΟΠΟΛΤΟΣ
TOMATO PASTE

Pork with Peppers

Serves 4
Preparation time 15 minutes
Cooking time 1½ hours

1 cup (250 ml / 8 fl oz) **olive oil**

2¼ lb (1 kg) boneless **pork shoulder**, cut into serving pieces

4 **onions**, coarsely chopped

3 **garlic cloves**, halved

2 tablespoons **red wine vinegar**

14 oz (400 g) canned **chopped tomatoes**

6 **allspice berries**

2 **bay leaves**

½ teaspoon **cayenne pepper** (optional)

salt and **pepper**

2¼ lb (1 kg) long **Florina** or **red bell peppers**, halved and seeded

Heat half the oil in a wide, shallow pan. Add the meat and cook over medium heat, turning occasionally, for 8–10 minutes, until lightly browned.

Add the onions, garlic, vinegar, tomatoes, allspice berries, bay leaves, and cayenne, if using, and season with salt and pepper. Stir well, reduce the heat, cover, and simmer for about 1 hour, or until the meat is tender.

Meanwhile, heat the remaining oil in a skillet or frying pan. Add the peppers and cook over low heat, turning occasionally, for 8 minutes, or until softened. Remove from the skillet and drain on paper towels. When they are cool enough to handle, peel off the skins and put the flesh into the pan, around and between the pieces of meat. Do not stir. Simmer for 15 minutes, or until the liquid has reduced. Serve hot.

Pork Skewers with Yogurt and Tomato Sauce

Serves 4
Preparation time 1 hour (including soaking)
Cooking time 30 minutes

2¼ lb (1 kg) **boneless pork**, cubed

pinch of **dried oregano**

pepper

olive oil, for brushing

8 **Pita breads** (p 148)

5 tablespoons (70 g / 2¾ oz) **butter**, melted

1½ cups (350 ml / 12 fl oz) **beef stock**

2¼ cups (500 ml / 18 fl oz) strained plain or thick **Greek yogurt**

pinch of **cayenne pepper**

FOR THE TOMATO SAUCE

3 tablespoons (40 g / 1½ oz) **butter**

1 **garlic clove**, finely chopped

1½ cups (350 ml / 12 fl oz) puréed fresh **tomatoes**

1 teaspoon **sugar**

pinch of **cayenne pepper**

pepper

Soak 8 wooden skewers in cold water for 30 minutes before using, so they don't burn.

Thread the cubes of pork onto the wooden skewers, put them on a platter, sprinkle with oregano, season with pepper, and brush with olive oil. Cover and leave in the refrigerator until required.

To make the sauce, melt the butter in a pan. Add the garlic and cook over low heat, stirring frequently, for 1–2 minutes. Add the tomatoes, sugar, and cayenne, season with pepper, and simmer for 5–10 minutes, or until thickened. Remove from the heat and let cool, then chill in the refrigerator.

An hour before serving, preheat the broiler (grill) or light the barbecue. Brush both sides of the Pita breads with the melted butter and broil (grill) them for a couple of minutes under the broiler, or grill over charcoal. Keep warm.

Cook the kabobs (kebabs) under the broiler or grill over charcoal for 10–15 minutes, or until cooked through, brushing with oil and turning frequently.

Meanwhile, heat the beef stock and the tomato sauce in separate pans. Cut the Pita breads into pieces and divide among individual plates. Spoon 5–6 tablespoons hot beef stock into each plate and spread 2–3 tablespoons yogurt on top. Slide the meat off 2 skewers onto each plate and spoon 3–4 tablespoons tomato sauce over the meat. Sprinkle with pepper and cayenne. Serve immediately.

Pork with Beans

Serves 6
Preparation time 12½ hours (including soaking)
Cooking time 3¼ hours

4½ lb (2 kg) boned and rolled **pork loin**

4–6 **garlic cloves**, sliced

4 tablespoons **olive oil**

4 tablespoons freshly squeezed **lemon juice**

salt and **pepper**

1 lb 2 oz (500 g) **dried lima (butter) beans**, soaked overnight in cold water to cover and drained

1 **bay leaf**

1 **onion**, studded with 3 **cloves**

2 **fresh parsley sprigs**

1 **carrot**

½ teaspoon **black peppercorns**

4 tablespoons **clarified butter**

1 large **onion**, finely chopped

2 tablespoons finely chopped **fresh parsley**

Preheat the oven to 325°F (160°C / Gas Mark 3).

Make small cuts all over the pork and insert the garlic slices. Put the pork into a deep ovenproof dish just large enough to hold it. Rub the meat with the oil, lemon juice, salt, and pepper. Pour in 1 cup (250 ml / 8 fl oz) water, cover with aluminum foil, and roast, occasionally basting with the cooking juices, for about 3 hours.

Meanwhile, put the beans into a large pan, pour in water to cover, and add the bay leaf, the whole onion, parsley, carrot, and peppercorns. Bring to a boil, skim off any scum, cover, and cook for 1–1½ hours, until the beans are soft.

Remove the pork from the dish, reserving the juices, and keep warm.

Melt the butter in a large pan. Add the chopped onion and cook over low heat, stirring occasionally, for 5 minutes, until softened. Strain the reserved cooking juices into the pan, cover, and simmer for 10 minutes, or until the onion is tender.

Drain the beans, discarding the flavorings, and mix with the onion. Simmer for a few minutes more until the beans are glazed. Slice the pork and serve hot with the beans, sprinkled with the chopped parsley.

Veal with Prunes and Almonds

Serves 4
Preparation time 12 hours (including marinating and soaking)
Cooking time 1¾ hours

1 lb 2 oz (500 g) **prunes**, pitted (stoned)

2 cups (450 ml / 16 fl oz) **Mavrodaphne** or other **sweet red wine**

3¼ lb (1.5 kg) **boneless stewing veal**, cut into 1½-inch (4-cm) cubes

1 **fresh rosemary sprig**

2 **garlic cloves**, halved

½ cup (120 ml / 4 fl oz) **olive oil**

salt and **pepper**

¾ cup (80 g / 3 oz) **blanched almonds**

½ teaspoon chopped **fresh rosemary**

rice or **mashed potatoes** and **carrots**, to serve

Put the prunes into a bowl, pour in ½ cup (120 ml / 4 fl oz) of the wine, and let soak for 6 hours.

Put the veal into a bowl, pour in the remaining wine, add the rosemary sprig and garlic, and let marinate in the refrigerator overnight.

The next day, drain the meat and pat dry. Reserve the wine but discard the rosemary sprig and garlic.

Heat the oil in a heavy pan. Add the meat and cook over medium heat, stirring frequently, for 8–10 minutes, until browned all over. Add the reserved wine, season with salt and pepper, cover, and simmer for 45 minutes, until the meat is half cooked.

Meanwhile, preheat the oven to 350°F (180°C / Gas Mark 4). Put the almonds into a nonstick skillet or frying pan and cook over medium heat, stirring constantly, for 1–2 minutes, or until lightly golden, then remove from the heat. Be careful not to burn them.

Transfer the meat and its cooking liquid to an ovenproof dish and add the almonds, chopped rosemary, and the prunes with their wine. Cover with aluminum foil and bake for about 45 minutes, or until the meat is meltingly tender. Serve accompanied by rice or mashed potatoes and carrots.

Meat-stuffed Eggplants

Serves 4
Preparation time 2–3 hours (including salting and cooling)
Cooking time 1¾ hours

4 **eggplants** (aubergines), 2¼ lb (1 kg), halved lengthwise

salt and **pepper**

1 cup (250 ml / 8 fl oz) **olive oil**

3 **scallions** (spring onions), finely chopped

1 **onion**, grated

1 lb 2 oz (500 g) **ground (minced) beef**

1 lb 2 oz (500 g) peeled, seeded, and chopped fresh or canned **tomatoes**

½ cup (25 g / 1 oz) finely chopped **fresh parsley**

1 **egg white**

2 **egg yolks**, lightly beaten

1 cup (120 g / 4 oz) **grated kefalotiri** or **Parmesan cheese**

2 **tomatoes**, thinly sliced

½ cup (120 ml / 4 fl oz) **hot water**

FOR THE WHITE SAUCE

1½ cups (350 ml / 12 fl oz) **milk**

3 tablespoons (40 g /1½ oz) **butter**

3 tablespoons **all-purpose (plain) flour**

pinch of **ground nutmeg**

salt and **white pepper**

Make 2 or 3 slashes in the flesh of each eggplant (aubergine) half with a knife. Sprinkle liberally with salt and let drain in a colander for 1–2 hours. Rinse under cold running water and squeeze out any excess moisture.

Heat half the oil in a skillet. Add the eggplants and cook over medium heat, turning occasionally, for 6–8 minutes. Drain on paper towels, then transfer to an ovenproof dish, flesh side up.

Heat the remaining oil in a pan. Add the scallions (spring onions) and onion and cook over low heat, stirring occasionally, for 5 minutes. Stir in the beef and cook, breaking up the meat with a spoon, for about 10 minutes, until lightly browned. Add the tomatoes and parsley, season with salt and pepper, and mix well. Reduce the heat, cover, and simmer for 10 minutes, until the sauce has reduced. Let cool.

Meanwhile, make the white sauce. Bring the milk just to a boil, then remove from the heat. Melt the butter in a heavy nonstick pan, stir in the flour, and cook, stirring frequently, for 1 minute. Remove from the heat and gradually pour in the milk, stirring constantly until the mixture is smooth. Return the sauce to medium heat and simmer, stirring constantly, for about 15 minutes, until thickened and smooth. Remove from the heat and season with nutmeg, salt, and white pepper.

Preheat the oven to 350°F (180°C / Gas Mark 4). Lightly beat the egg white and stir it into the meat mixture. With the back of a large spoon, press a cavity in the center of each eggplant half and divide the filling evenly into each one, heaping it up.

Fold the egg yolks and half the grated cheese into the white sauce and spread the sauce evenly over the eggplants. Garnish with half the tomato slices, sprinkle with the remaining cheese, and season with pepper. Pour the hot water into the dish and bake for about 1 hour, or until the tops are golden.

Moussaka

Serves 6
Preparation time 2 hours (including salting, cooling, and standing)
Cooking time 1 hour 50 minutes

4½ lb (2 kg) **eggplants** (aubergines), cut into ½-inch (1-cm) slices

salt and **pepper**

½ cup (120 ml / 4 fl oz) **olive oil**

1 **onion**, grated

2 **garlic cloves**, sliced

1 lb 2 oz (500 g) lean **ground (minced) beef**

2 cups (450 ml / 16 fl oz) peeled fresh or canned **tomatoes**, puréed

¼ teaspoon **ground allspice**

½ teaspoon **sugar**

1 **egg white**, lightly beaten

5 tablespoons finely chopped **fresh parsley**

butter, for greasing

5 tablespoons fine **dried bread crumbs**

scant 1 cup (100 g / 3½ oz) **grated kefalotiri**, **Parmesan**, or **regato cheese**

5 tablespoons **heavy (double) cream**

3 **egg yolks**, lightly beaten

FOR THE WHITE SAUCE

3 cups (750 ml / 1¼ pints) **milk**

3 tablespoons (40 g /1½ oz) **butter**

3 tablespoons **all-purpose (plain) flour**

pinch of **ground nutmeg**

salt and **white pepper**

Sprinkle the eggplant (aubergine) slices with salt and let drain in a colander for 1 hour. Rinse, squeeze out the excess water, and pat dry.

Heat half the oil in a skillet or frying pan. Add the eggplants and cook over medium heat, turning occasionally, for 6–8 minutes, until lightly browned on both sides. Drain on paper towels.

Heat the remaining oil in a heavy pan. Add the onion and garlic and cook over low heat, stirring occasionally, for 5 minutes, until softened. Increase the heat to medium, add the ground (minced) beef, and cook, stirring and breaking up the meat with the spoon, for 10 minutes, until lightly browned. Add the tomatoes, allspice, and sugar, and season with salt and pepper. Reduce the heat and simmer for 15–20 minutes, or until all the liquid has evaporated. Let cool, then fold in the egg white and parsley.

Preheat the oven to 400°F (200°C / Gas Mark 6) and grease a deep ovenproof dish, 10 × 14 inches (25 × 35 cm), with butter and sprinkle with 2 tablespoons of the bread crumbs. Cover the base of the dish with half the prepared eggplant slices, overlapping them slightly. Spread half the meat mixture on top and sprinkle with half the grated cheese and 2 tablespoons of the remaining bread crumbs. Cover with the remaining eggplant slices, spread the remaining meat mixture on top, and sprinkle with the remaining cheese and remaining bread crumbs. (At this point, the dish may be covered and frozen. Thaw before baking.)

Make the white sauce according to the instructions on page 124. Stir the cream and egg yolks into the sauce and spread it evenly over the surface of the dish. Bake for about 50 minutes, or until the top is golden brown. Remove from the oven and let stand for 15 minutes before serving.

Pastitsio

⬠

Serves 4
Preparation time 1 hour (including cooling)
Cooking time 2 hours 10 minutes

⅔ cup (150 ml / ¼ pint) **olive oil**

1 **onion**, grated

1 lb 2 oz (500 g) **ground (minced) beef**

1 cup (250 ml / 8 fl oz) puréed peeled fresh or canned **tomatoes**

1 tablespoon **tomato paste** (purée)

pinch of **ground cinnamon** (optional)

½ teaspoon **sugar**

3 tablespoons finely chopped **fresh parsley**

salt and **pepper**

1 **egg white**, lightly beaten

scant 1 cup (100 g / 3½ oz) **grated kefalograviera** or other **semi-hard cheese** such as Cheddar

11 oz (300 g) **thick tube-shaped pasta**, such as macaroni or ziti

4 tablespoons **melted butter**, plus extra for brushing

2 tablespoons fine **bread crumbs**

2 cups (225 g / 8 oz) grated **Gruyère cheese**

3 **egg yolks**, lightly beaten

FOR THE WHITE SAUCE

3 cups (750 ml / 1¼ pints) **milk**

3 tablespoons (40 g /1½ oz) **butter**

3 tablespoons **all-purpose (plain) flour**

pinch of **ground nutmeg**

salt and **white pepper**

Heat ½ cup (120 ml / 4 fl oz) of the oil in a large pan. Add the onion and cook over low heat, stirring occasionally, for 5 minutes, until softened. Increase the heat to medium, add the ground (minced) beef, and cook, stirring and breaking up the meat with the spoon, for 10–15 minutes, until lightly browned. Stir in the tomatoes, tomato paste (purée), cinnamon, if using, sugar, and parsley and season with salt and pepper. Reduce the heat and simmer for 15–20 minutes, or until the liquid has reduced. Remove from the heat and let cool for 5 minutes. Fold in the egg white and ½ cup (50 g / 2 oz) of the kefalograviera or Cheddar cheese. Taste and adjust the seasoning if necessary.

Bring a large pan of water to a boil, stir in salt and the remaining oil, add the pasta, and cook for 8–10 minutes, or until al dente. Drain and toss with the melted butter, then let cool.

Meanwhile, make the white sauce according to the instructions on page 124.

Preheat the oven to 350°F (180°C / Gas Mark 4), brush a 10 × 14-inch (25 × 35-cm) ovenproof dish with melted butter and sprinkle with the bread crumbs.

Stir the Gruyère cheese into the cooled pasta. Fold the egg yolks and the remaining kefalograviera or Cheddar into the white sauce.

Line the base of the prepared dish with half the pasta mixture and spread the meat mixture on top. Cover with the remaining pasta and pour the white sauce over it. Bake for about 1 hour, or until the top is golden brown. Let the dish stand for 15 minutes before cutting into serving pieces. Serve hot.

Lamb Baked with Orzo

Serves 6
Preparation time 30 minutes
Cooking time 3¼ hours

½ cup (120 ml / 4 fl oz) **olive oil**

3¼ lb (1.5 kg) **stewing lamb**, trimmed and cut into serving pieces

3 cups (750 ml / 1¼ pints) puréed peeled fresh **tomatoes** or puréed canned tomatoes

4 **garlic cloves**, sliced

½ teaspoon **sugar**

salt and **pepper**

4 tablespoons (50 g / 2 oz) **butter**

1 lb 2 oz (500 g) **orzo pasta**

3 cups (750 ml / 1¼ pints) **hot water**

1 **tomato**, thinly sliced

½ cup (50 g / 2 oz) **grated kefalotiri** or **Parmesan cheese**, plus extra to serve

Heat the oil in a large pan. Add the meat and cook over medium heat, turning occasionally, for 8–10 minutes, until lightly browned all over. Add the puréed tomatoes, garlic, and sugar, season with salt and pepper, cover, and simmer for 1 hour.

Meanwhile, melt the butter in a nonstick skillet or frying pan. Add the orzo and cook over high heat, stirring constantly, for 5 minutes, until lightly golden. Transfer the orzo to a large ovenproof dish or divide among 6 individual dishes. (In Greece, a special clay pot called a *giouvetsi* is used for this dish.)

Preheat the oven to 350°F (180°C / Gas Mark 4). Put the pieces of lamb on top of the orzo and pour the tomato sauce over them. Carefully add the hot water and cover the dish with aluminum foil. Bake for 1½ hours.

Remove from the oven and put the tomato slices on top of the lamb, sprinkle with the cheese, and season with pepper. Return to the oven and bake, adding a little more water if necessary, for 30 minutes more, until the liquid has almost all been absorbed and the pasta is al dente. Serve immediately with extra grated cheese.

Note: Veal, beef, pork, chicken, or even shellfish can be substituted for the lamb, adjusting the cooking times as necessary.

Leg of Lamb in Paper

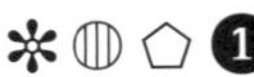

Serves 6
Preparation time 20 minutes
Cooking time 2½ hours

3–4 **garlic cloves**, thinly sliced

salt and **pepper**

pinch of **dried oregano** (optional)

1 **leg of lamb**, about 6 lb 10 oz (3 kg)

2 tablespoons freshly squeezed **lemon juice**

olive oil, for brushing

roasted potatoes and **mustard**, to serve

Preheat the oven to 350°F (180°C / Gas Mark 4).

Season the slices of garlic with salt and pepper and sprinkle with oregano, if using, pressing it on with your fingers. Using a sharp knife, make 20–25 incisions in the surface of the meat and insert the seasoned garlic. Rub the meat with the lemon juice and brush with oil.

Cut a piece of baking parchment large enough to hold the meat and brush with oil. Wrap it around the leg of lamb and secure with kitchen string. Put the lamb into a roasting pan and brush the outside of the parcel with a little oil. Roast for 2½ hours.

Unwrap, cut into slices, and serve hot with roasted potatoes and mustard.

Stuffed Lamb Roll in Grape Leaves

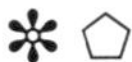

Serves 6
Preparation time 30 minutes
Cooking time 3¼ hours

- 1 boned and rolled **leg of lamb**, about 4½ lb (2 kg)
- **salt** and **pepper**
- 1 lb 2 oz (500 g) **spinach**, coarse stalks removed, cut into thick strips
- ½ cup (120 ml / 4 fl oz) **olive oil**
- 1¾ cups (200 g / 7 oz) coarsely grated **halloumi** or **mozzarella cheese**
- 2 tablespoons finely chopped **fresh mint**
- 5 oz (150 g) **grape (vine) leaves**, blanched
- 5 tablespoons **dry white wine**
- 1 tablespoon **cornstarch** (cornflour)
- buttered seasonal **vegetables**, to serve

Preheat the oven to 350°F (180°C / Gas Mark 4). Unroll the meat, lay it out flat on a work surface, and season with salt and pepper.

Rinse the spinach in cold water and cook over low heat in just the water clinging to the leaves after rinsing, for 4–5 minutes, until wilted. Drain well.

Heat half the oil in a pan. Add the spinach and cook, stirring frequently, for 4–5 minutes. Spread it out on top of the meat. Combine the cheese and mint in a bowl and sprinkle the mixture down the middle of the meat. Roll up and tie securely with kitchen string. Brush a piece of wax (greaseproof) paper large enough to enclose the meat with some of the remaining oil and line it with 2–3 layers of grape (vine) leaves. Drizzle with the remaining oil, season with a little salt and pepper, and place the meat roll on top. Wrap the paper around it and secure with kitchen string.

Put the parcel into an ovenproof dish just large enough to hold it, pour in ½ cup (120 ml / 4 fl oz) water, and bake for 3 hours. Remove from the oven and open the parcel while it is still in the dish. Remove the meat and let rest for 10 minutes before slicing.

Meanwhile, pour the wine and the cooking juices into a small pan and cook over medium heat for 5 minutes. Mix the cornstarch to a paste with 2 tablespoons water in a bowl, add to the pan, and cook, stirring constantly, until thickened. Season with salt and pepper and pour the sauce over the sliced meat. Serve immediately with buttered seasonal vegetables.

Note: Lamb is cooked this way in many parts of Greece, and each region uses its own local cheese in the stuffing—graviera in Crete, ladotiri in Lesvos, kalathaki in Limnos, kefalograviera in Epirus, and formaela in Sterea Ellada.

Pies & Breads

Cheese Pie

Makes 16 small squares
Preparation time 2 hours 35 minutes (including resting)
Cooking time 40 minutes

½ cup (120 ml / 4 fl oz) melted **clarified butter**

2 **egg whites**

½ cup (120 ml / 4 fl oz) **light (single) cream** or **evaporated milk**

1½ lb (700 g) **feta cheese**, crumbled

pepper

FOR THE PHYLLO DOUGH

4½ cups (500 g / 1 lb 2 oz) **all-purpose (plain) flour**, plus extra for dusting

2 teaspoons **salt**

2 teaspoons **baking powder**

2 tablespoons **olive oil**

1 tablespoon **red wine vinegar**

1 cup (250 ml / 8 fl oz) **warm water**

cornstarch (cornflour), for dusting

For the phyllo dough (filo pastry), lightly dust a baking pan with flour and set aside. Sift together the flour, salt, and baking powder into a bowl. Make a well in the center and pour in the oil, vinegar, and water. Using your hands, gradually draw the flour from the sides of the well into the liquid and mix well. Knead lightly to form a soft, elastic dough, adding a little more water if necessary.

Divide into 12 small balls, and place them side by side in the pan. Cover with plastic wrap (cling film) or a damp dish towel, and let rest for 1–2 hours. Roll out each ball on a work surface lightly dusted with cornstarch (cornflour) into 12 × 16-inch (30 × 40-cm) sheets.

Preheat the oven to 350°F (180°C / Gas Mark 4) and brush a large rectangular baking pan with a little of the melted butter.

Beat the egg whites with the cream or evaporated milk in a bowl, then stir in the cheese.

Carefully place half the phyllo sheets one on top of the other in the prepared pan, brushing each sheet with melted butter. Spread the filling evenly on top and season with pepper. Cover with the remaining phyllo sheets, brushing each with melted butter. Score the pie into wide strips and bake for 40 minutes, or until the top is golden brown.

Serve hot, cut into bite-size pieces if you want to eat it the way they do in Thessaloniki.

Note: You can use ready-made phyllo (filo) sheets in place of homemade, or substitute with puff pastry.

ΧΙΟΣ
ΟΥΖΟ

Eggplant Spirals

Makes 12 spirals
Preparation time 1 hour
Cooking time 1 hour

⅔ cup (150 ml / ¼ pint) **olive oil**

1 lb 2 oz (500 g) ready-made **phyllo** (filo) or 1 x quantity **homemade Phyllo Dough** (filo pastry), p 138

FOR THE FILLING

4½ lb (2 kg) **eggplants** (aubergines)

½ cup (120 ml / 4 fl oz) **olive oil**

1 large **onion**, grated

1 tablespoon **balsamic vinegar**

4 oz (120 g) **feta cheese**, crumbled (optional)

½ cup (25 g / 1 oz) finely chopped **fresh parsley** or **mint**

½ cup (120 ml / 4 fl oz) **light (single) cream** or **evaporated milk**

4 **eggs**, lightly beaten

2 tablespoons **bread crumbs**

salt and **pepper**

First, make the filling. Preheat the broiler (grill). Broil (grill) the eggplants (aubergines), turning frequently, for 5–8 minutes, or until the skins are charred and the flesh is softened. Remove from the heat and hold each eggplant briefly under cold running water until cool enough to handle, then peel. Do not let the unpeeled eggplants cool completely or the flesh will turn black. Cut the eggplant flesh into pieces and transfer to a bowl.

Heat the oil in a pan. Add the onion and cook over low heat, stirring occasionally, for 5 minutes, until softened. Add the eggplants, vinegar, cheese, if using, parsley or mint, cream or evaporated milk, eggs, and bread crumbs. Season with salt and pepper, mix well, then remove from the heat.

Preheat the oven to 350°F (180°C / Gas Mark 4) and brush a large cookie sheet (baking tray) with oil.

If using homemade, roll out each piece of phyllo dough (filo pastry) into a thin sheet. Lay out 1 sheet of phyllo with the short edge nearest to you. Brush the top half with oil, fold over the bottom half, and brush with oil again. Put 3–4 tablespoons of filling on the long edge and roll up. Wind the roll into a loose spiral. Make more spirals in the same way until all the phyllo and filling are used.

Arrange the spirals on the prepared cookie sheet, seam side down. Brush the rolls with the remaining oil and bake for 40–50 minutes, or until golden brown. Serve immediately or at room temperature.

Spinach and Cheese Pie

Makes 8 pieces
Preparation time 30 minutes
Cooking time 1 hour

½ cup (120 ml / 4 fl oz) **olive oil**

1 lb 2 oz (500 g) ready-made **phyllo** (filo) or 1 x quantity homemade **Phyllo Dough** (filo pastry), p 138

2¼ lb (1 kg) **spinach**, coarse stalks removed, chopped

salt and **pepper**

1 cup (100 g / 3½ oz) finely chopped **scallions** (spring onions)

½ cup (15 g / ½ oz) finely chopped **fresh dill**

½ cup (25 g / 1 oz) finely chopped **fresh parsley**

1 lb 2 oz (500 g) **feta cheese**, crumbled

4 tablespoons **milk**

3–4 **eggs**, lightly beaten

4 tablespoons melted **clarified butter**

Preheat the oven to 350°F (180°C / Gas Mark 4) and brush a 14-inch (35-cm) baking pan with oil. If using homemade, roll the phyllo dough (filo pastry) into thin 18-inch (46-cm) rounds.

Sprinkle the spinach with a little salt and rub with your fingers. Rinse, drain, and squeeze out the excess water. Alternatively, blanch it for 1 minute, drain, and squeeze out the excess water.

Combine the spinach, scallions (spring onions), dill, parsley, cheese, milk, eggs, and melted butter in a bowl and season with pepper.

Lay half the phyllo sheets in the prepared pan, one on top of the other, brushing each with oil. Spread the spinach filling evenly on top and cover with the remaining phyllo sheets, brushing each with oil. Roll up the overhanging phyllo neatly around the pan. Score into 8 serving pieces, and brush the top with oil. Sprinkle with a little water and bake for 1 hour, or until golden brown. Serve warm or at room temperature.

Ruffled Milk Pie

Makes 1 large pie
Preparation time 15 minutes
Cooking time 1 hour

6 tablespoons melted **clarified butter**

8–9 ready-made **phyllo (filo) sheets**

¼ teaspoon **ground cinnamon**, plus extra for dusting (optional)

3 cups (750 ml / 1¼ pints) **milk**

6 **eggs**

generous 1 cup (225 g / 8 oz) **superfine (caster) sugar**

1 teaspoon **vanilla extract**

confectioners' (icing) sugar, for dusting

Preheat the oven to 350°F (180°C / Gas Mark 4) and brush a 14-inch (35-cm) round baking pan with some of the melted butter.

Lay 1 sheet of phyllo on a work surface with the long edge toward you. Loosely ruffle it by pushing the short ends toward each other with your hands to create a long concertina shape, then place it upright in a loose spiral in the center of the prepared pan. Ruffle the remaining sheets of phyllo in the same way and continue the spiral until the base of the pan is filled with phyllo ruffles. Using a pastry brush, dab the melted butter on all the surfaces of the phyllo. Sprinkle with the ground cinnamon and bake for 25–30 minutes, or until golden brown.

Meanwhile, pour the milk into a pan and bring to just below boiling point, then remove from the heat. Beat the eggs with the sugar in a bowl. Gradually pour in the milk, a little at a time, beating constantly. Add the vanilla and spoon the egg mixture over the baked phyllo, covering all the surfaces evenly. Return the pan to the oven and bake for 25–30 minutes more, or until the filling has set. Dust with confectioners' sugar and extra ground cinnamon, if using, and serve immediately.

Tomato Flatbread

Makes 1 large flatbread
Preparation time 1¼ hours (including rising)
Cooking time 20–25 minutes

1¼ cups (250 g / 9 oz) **all-purpose (plain) flour**, plus extra for dusting

½ teaspoon **salt**

1½ teaspoons rapid-rise (fast-action) **dried yeast**

1 teaspoon **mixed dried herbs**, such as oregano, thyme, or mint

1 tablespoon **honey**

5 tablespoons **olive oil**, plus extra for brushing

½ cup (120 ml / 4 fl oz) **lukewarm water**

4 **garlic cloves**, thinly sliced

2 tablespoons **tomato paste** (purée)

2¼ lb (1 kg) **tomatoes**, peeled, seeded, and coarsely chopped

2 tablespoons **tomato ketchup**

1 teaspoon **Dijon mustard**

salt and **pepper**

1 teaspoon **dried oregano**

1 teaspoon **dried thyme**

Sift together the flour and salt into a bowl, stir in the yeast and mixed herbs, and make a well in the center. Add the honey, 1 tablespoon of the oil, and the lukewarm water and incorporate the dry ingredients to form a soft elastic dough. Brush with oil, cover, and let rise in a warm place for 30 minutes, or until doubled in volume.

Meanwhile, heat the remaining oil in a pan. Add the garlic and cook over low heat for 1–2 minutes. Mix the tomato paste (purée) with 4 tablespoons water. Add the tomato paste mixture, tomatoes, ketchup, and mustard to the pan, and season with salt and pepper. Increase the heat to medium, and cook for 3 minutes, or until slightly thickened.

Preheat the oven to 400°F (200°C / Gas Mark 6).

Roll out the dough on a lightly floured work surface and pat into a 12-inch (30-cm) pizza pan. Spread the tomato sauce evenly over the surface, leaving a generous ¾-inch (2-cm) margin around the edge. Sprinkle with the dried herbs and let rise for 10 minutes.

Bake for 15–20 minutes, or until browned. Serve immediately.

Pita Bread

Makes 6 pita breads
Preparation time 2 hours (including rising)
Cooking time 15 minutes

3 cups (350 g / 12 oz) **all-purpose (plain) flour**

1 teaspoon **salt**

1 tablespoon **dried yeast**

2 teaspoons **sugar**

2 tablespoons **olive oil**, plus extra for brushing

¾ cup (175 ml / 6 fl oz) **lukewarm water**

cornmeal, for dusting

Combine the flour, salt, yeast, and sugar in a large bowl. Add the oil and lukewarm water and knead lightly until the dough comes away from the sides of the bowl. Leave in a warm place to rise for about 30 minutes.

Divide the dough into six pieces and roll out into 8-inch (20-cm) rounds, ¼-inch (5 mm) thick. Dust lightly with cornmeal, cover, and let rise for 5 minutes.

Score the pita breads crosswise with the tines of a fork or a pastry wheel, taking care not to cut through. Brush a heavy nonstick skillet or frying pan with oil and fry the breads over high heat for 3 minutes on each side, until browned in several places but not completely cooked. Remove and immediately place in airtight bags to keep them moist. Let cool completely and broil (grill), bake in a hot oven, or fry to reheat.

Cinnamon Twists

Makes 8–10 twists
Preparation time 2¾ hours (including rising)
Cooking time 25 minutes

FOR THE DOUGH

4 tablespoons **evaporated milk**

4 tablespoons (50 g / 2 oz) **butter**

4 tablespoons **superfine (caster) sugar**

½ teaspoon **salt**

1 oz (25 g) **fresh yeast** or 1 tablespoon dried yeast

5 tablespoons **lukewarm water**

2 **eggs**

4½ cups (500 g / 1 lb 2 oz) strong **white bread flour,** plus extra for dusting

2–3 tablespoons melted **butter**, plus extra for brushing

FOR THE FILLING

2 tablespoons **ground cinnamon**

4 tablespoons **superfine (caster) sugar**

4 tablespoons (50 g / 2 oz) **butter**, softened

For the dough, put the evaporated milk, butter, sugar, and salt into a small pan and cook over medium heat, stirring occasionally, until the butter has melted and the sugar has dissolved. Remove from the heat and let cool slightly.

If using fresh yeast, mash it with the lukewarm water in a bowl to a smooth paste. If using dried yeast, pour the lukewarm water into a bowl, sprinkle the yeast over the surface, and let stand for 10–15 minutes until frothy, then stir to a smooth paste.

Beat the eggs and stir them into the butter mixture, together with the dissolved yeast and half the flour, stirring until the batter is smooth. Gradually add more flour and knead until the dough is pliable and smooth. It should be slightly softer than regular bread dough. Divide it into 3 pieces, cover, and let rise in a warm place for 1½ hours, or until doubled in volume.

Roll out each piece of dough on a lightly floured work surface into an 8 × 12-inch (20 × 30-cm) rectangle.

For the filling, combine the cinnamon and sugar in a bowl. Spread half the softened butter on 1 dough rectangle and sprinkle with half the cinnamon and sugar mixture. Put the second sheet of dough on top, spread with the remaining softened butter, and sprinkle with the remaining cinnamon and sugar mixture. Put the third sheet of dough on top and brush with melted butter. Cover and let rise for 10 minutes.

Meanwhile, brush a cookie sheet (baking tray) with melted butter. Cut the stacked dough lengthwise into generous ¾-inch (2-cm) strips with a pizza cutter. Twist each strip 2–3 times, roll into spirals, and place on the prepared cookie sheet. Brush with melted butter, cover, and let rise until doubled in volume.

Meanwhile, preheat the oven to 400°F (200°C / Gas Mark 6). Brush the twists with melted butter and bake for 15–20 minutes, or until lightly golden. Serve warm.

Sesame Bread Rings

Makes 20–25 rings
Preparation time 25 hours (including rising)
Cooking time 10–15 minutes

½ oz (15 g) **fresh yeast** or 1½ teaspoons dried yeast

1¼ cups (300 ml / ½ pint) **warm water**

4 cups (500 g / 1 lb 2 oz) **all-purpose (plain) flour**, plus extra for dusting

1 teaspoon **salt**

¼ cup (50 g / 2 oz) **superfine (caster) sugar**

2 tablespoons **vegetable oil**

1 cup (175 g / 6 oz) **sesame seeds**

Dissolve half the yeast in ½ cup (120 ml / 4 fl oz) of the warm water and stir in 3–4 tablespoons of the flour. Cover and set aside in a warm place for 24 hours.

Shortly before making the dough, dissolve the remaining yeast in ½ cup (120 ml / 4 fl oz) warm water, stir in 3–4 tablespoons of the flour, and let rise for 15 minutes.

Sift the remaining flour with the salt into a large mixing bowl and make a well in the center. Pour in both yeast mixtures, the sugar, oil, and remaining water. Gradually incorporate the flour into the liquid until a sticky dough forms. Knead the dough on a floured work surface for about 15 minutes, until smooth and elastic. Cover and leave to rise until doubled in size.

Punch down the dough and roll out into an oblong about ¾-inch (2-cm) thick. With a sharp, floured knife, cut the dough lengthwise into ¾-inch (2-cm) strips. Roll the strips evenly into 14-inch (35-cm) strands. Brush with water and roll in the sesame seeds until completely coated. Pinch the ends together to form rings and arrange on cookie sheets (baking trays) lined with baking parchment. Cover and let rise for about 20 minutes.

Meanwhile, preheat the oven to 425°F (220°C / Gas Mark 7). Bake for 10–15 minutes, or until golden brown on the outside, but soft on the inside. Cool on a wire rack and serve warm, preferably on the same day.

Cookies & Cakes

Christmas Honey-dipped Cookies

▼

Makes 20–25 cookies
Preparation time 30 minutes
Cooking time 30 minutes

4 cups (450 g / 1 lb) **all-purpose (plain) flour**, plus extra for dusting

½ teaspoon **baking soda** (bicarbonate of soda)

1 teaspoon **baking powder**

¾ cup (175 ml / 6 fl oz) **olive oil**

4 tablespoons (50 g / 2 oz) **butter**, softened

½ cup (100 g / 3½ oz) **superfine (caster) sugar**

½ cup (120 ml / 4 fl oz) freshly squeezed **orange juice**

2 tablespoons **brandy**

1 tablespoon grated **orange zest**

1 cup (120 g / 4 oz) **walnuts**, finely chopped

1 teaspoon **ground cinnamon**

¼ teaspoon **ground cloves**

FOR THE SYRUP

1 cup (250 ml / 8 fl oz) **honey**

1 cup (200 g / 7 oz) **superfine (caster) sugar**

Sift together the flour, baking soda (bicarbonate of soda), and baking powder into a bowl and make a well in the center. Put the oil, butter, sugar, orange juice, brandy, and orange zest into a food processor and process at high speed. Pour the mixture into the well and gradually incorporate the dry ingredients. Mix gently to combine, without kneading, to form a soft dough.

Preheat the oven to 350°F (180°C / Gas Mark 4). Roll out the dough on a lightly floured work surface to ½ inch (1 cm) thick and stamp out rounds, ovals, or squares with cookie cutters. Put the cookies onto ungreased cookie sheets (baking trays) and crosshatch the tops with the tines of a fork. Bake for about 30 minutes, or until golden brown.

Meanwhile, make the syrup. Put the honey and sugar into a large pan, pour in 1 cup (250 ml / 8 fl oz) water, and bring to a boil, stirring until the sugar has dissolved. Simmer for 5 minutes, skimming off the froth. Pour the syrup over the cookies as soon as they come out of the oven. When all the syrup has been absorbed, turn them over, and let cool completely.

Combine the walnuts, cinnamon, and cloves in a bowl and sprinkle the mixture over the cookies. Transfer to a platter and cover with plastic wrap (cling film) until ready to serve. They keep well, covered, at room temperature for up to 3 weeks.

Apple-filled Cookies

Makes 30 cookies
Preparation time 1 hour (including chilling)
Cooking time 35 minutes

FOR THE DOUGH

3½ cups (400 g / 14 oz) **self-rising (self-raising) flour**

1 cup (225 g / 8 oz) **butter**, chilled and diced

4–5 tablespoons **plain yogurt**

butter, for greasing

confectioners' (icing) sugar, for dusting

FOR THE FILLING

4 large **apples**, peeled and coarsely grated

2 tablespoons freshly squeezed **lemon juice**

4 tablespoons **superfine (caster) sugar**

½ teaspoon **ground cinnamon**, plus extra for dusting

½ teaspoon **ground cloves**

½ teaspoon freshly grated **nutmeg**

1 cup (120 g / 4 oz) **walnuts**, coarsely chopped

Sift the flour into a large bowl. Add the diced butter and rub it in with your fingertips until the mixture resembles coarse crumbs. Lightly stir in the yogurt and mix until the dough just begins to come together. It should feel crumbly. Do not knead, just gather all the crumbs from the side of the bowl into a ball, pressing them together with your hands. Cover and chill in the refrigerator for 30 minutes.

Meanwhile, make the filling. Put the apples, lemon juice, and sugar into a small pan and cook over low heat, stirring constantly, until all the liquid has evaporated. Remove from the heat and stir in the spices and walnuts.

Preheat the oven to 350°F (180°C / Gas Mark 4) and grease 1 or 2 large cookie sheets (baking trays) with butter.

Divide the dough into 30 pieces. Roll each piece into a ball, then press your thumb into the ball to form a large hollow. Spoon the filling into the hollows and press the dough over it to seal. Pat them down very gently. Put the balls, seam side down, on the prepared cookie sheets and bake for about 35 minutes, or until lightly golden.

Remove from the oven and sift a little confectioners' sugar and cinnamon on top, then let cool. They can be kept for 2–3 days at room temperature and for several months in the freezer.

Easter Cookies

Makes 60–80 cookies
Preparation time 30 minutes
Cooking time 20–30 minutes

1 cup (225 g / 8 oz) **butter**, softened, plus extra for greasing

1½ cups (300 g / 11 oz) **superfine (caster) sugar**

4 **eggs**

4 **egg yolks**

3 teaspoons **vanilla extract**

1 oz (25 g) **baking soda** (bicarbonate of soda)

½ cup (120 ml / 4 fl oz) **milk**

9 cups (1 kg / 2¼ lb) **all-purpose (plain) flour**

Preheat the oven to 400°F (200°C / Gas Mark 6) and grease a cookie sheet (baking tray) with butter.

Beat together the butter and sugar with an electric mixer. Beating constantly, add the eggs and 2 of the egg yolks, 1 at a time, then add the vanilla.

Fit the mixer with a dough hook. Combine the baking soda (bicarbonate of soda) and milk in a bowl. Beating constantly, add the milk mixture in 2–3 batches, alternating with the flour. Knead the mixture, adding flour as necessary to form a smooth, easy-to-handle dough.

Roll pieces of the dough into 8-inch (20-cm) long, finger-thick cylinders. Fold in half, twist, and put them on the prepared cookie sheet, spaced well apart. Beat the remaining egg yolks with 2 teaspoons water in a bowl and brush the cookies with the mixture. Bake for 20–30 minutes.

Chocolate and Wafer Mosaic

▼

Serves 12
Preparation time 2 hours (including chilling)

8 oz (225 g) **semisweet (plain) chocolate**, broken into pieces

5 tablespoons **milk**

5 tablespoons **brandy**

1 cup (225 g / 8 oz) **butter**, softened

1 cup (120 g / 4 oz) **confectioners' (icing) sugar**

¼ teaspoon **salt**

1 cup (120 g / 4 oz) **blanched almonds**, chopped and roasted

14 oz (400 g) **vanilla wafers**, coarsely chopped

1 cup (120 g / 4 oz) coarsely ground **walnuts**

FOR THE GLAZE (OPTIONAL)

8 oz (225 g) **semisweet (plain) chocolate**, broken into pieces

2 tablespoons **butter**

½ cup (60 g / 2¼ oz) **confectioners' (icing) sugar**

1 teaspoon **vanilla extract**

½ cup (120 ml / 4 fl oz) **milk**

Melt the chocolate in a heatproof bowl set over a pan of barely simmering water, then remove from the heat, and let cool.

Combine the milk and brandy in a bowl. Beat together the butter, sugar, and salt in another bowl with an electric mixer on medium speed.

Beating constantly at low speed, gradually add half the milk mixture and then the melted chocolate. Stir in the almonds. Sprinkle the wafers with the remaining milk mixture, then stir into the chocolate mixture. Chill in the refrigerator until thickened.

Roll the mixture into a thick cylinder, wrap in plastic wrap (cling film), and return to the refrigerator until ready to serve. Serve in slices. It keeps well for 1 week in the refrigerator and for 6 months in the freezer.

To make the chocolate glaze, if using, put the chocolate and butter into a pan and melt over very low heat or in a heatproof bowl set over a pan of barely simmering water. Stir in the sugar, vanilla, and as much milk as necessary to obtain a thin glaze, then spread it on the chocolate mosaic.

Hazelnut Cake

▼

Makes one 10-inch (25-cm) cake
Preparation time 15 minutes
Cooking time 1 hour

1 cup (225 g / 8 oz) soft **butter** or **margarine**, plus extra for greasing

3 cups (350 g / 12 oz) **self-rising (self-raising) flour**, plus extra for dusting

2 cups (400 g / 14 oz) **superfine (caster) sugar**

2 teaspoons **vanilla extract**

⅔ cup (150 ml / ¼ pint) **milk**

5 **eggs**

1 cup (120 g / 4 oz) **hazelnuts**, roasted and ground

confectioners' (icing) sugar, for dusting (or see Note)

Preheat the oven to 350°F (180°C / Gas Mark 4). Grease a 10-inch (25-cm) turban or ring mold with butter or margarine and lightly dust with flour.

Put the butter, flour, superfine (caster) sugar, vanilla, milk, and eggs into a bowl and mix lightly with a spoon, then beat with an electric mixer on high speed for 4 minutes, scraping the sides of the bowl frequently with a spatula, until doubled in volume and fluffy. Add the ground hazelnuts, a little at a time, lightly sprinkling them on the batter and folding in.

Pour the batter into the prepared mold, filling it to two-thirds of its depth. Bake for 1 hour, or until a wooden toothpick inserted into the center of the cake comes out clean.

Let cool in the mold for 5 minutes, then turn out onto a serving dish. Dust with confectioners' (icing) sugar while it is still warm. Store in an airtight container or freeze.

Note: You could use chocolate frosting (icing) in place of the confectioners' sugar, if desired.

Jam Tart

Makes one 10-inch (25-cm) tart
Preparation time 20 minutes
Cooking time 30–35 minutes

3 cups (350 g / 12 oz) **all-purpose (plain) flour**, plus extra for dusting

1 teaspoon **baking powder**

1 cup (225 g / 8 oz) **butter**

scant ½ cup (80 g / 3 oz) **superfine (caster) sugar**

2 **egg yolks**

2 tablespoons **brandy**

1 tablespoon grated **lemon zest** or 1 teaspoon **vanilla extract**

1¾ cups (500 g / 1 lb 2 oz) **apricot jam**, or other flavors as desired

Preheat the oven to 350°F (180°C / Gas Mark 4).

Sift together the flour and baking powder into a bowl. Beat together the butter and sugar in another bowl with an electric mixer until pale and fluffy. Beat in the egg yolks, brandy, and lemon zest or vanilla, then fold in the flour, and knead until smooth. Avoid overworking the dough.

Roll out two-thirds of the dough on a lightly floured work surface into a circle to fit the base and sides of a 10-inch (25-cm) tart pan. Spread the jam over the dough.

Roll out the remaining dough, cut into strips, and lay them over the top of the jam in a lattice pattern. Bake for 30–35 minutes, or until lightly golden.

Serve warm or at room temperature. Store, uncovered, in a cool, dry place for up to 1 week.

Pastries & Candies

Baklava

▼

Makes 30 pieces
Preparation time 1¼ hours
Cooking time 30–40 minutes

1 lb 2 oz (500 g) ready-made **phyllo** (filo) or 1 x quantity homemade **Phyllo Dough** (filo pastry), p 138

1½ cups (350 g / 12 oz) melted **clarified butter**, plus extra for brushing

2 cups (225 g / 8 oz) **almonds**, coarsely chopped

2 cups (225 g / 8 oz) **walnuts**, coarsely chopped

2 teaspoons **ground cinnamon**

½ teaspoon **ground cloves**

cloves, to decorate (optional)

FOR THE SYRUP

3 cups (600 g / 1 lb 5 oz) **superfine (caster) sugar**

½ cup (120 ml / 4 fl oz) **corn syrup** or **honey**

grated **zest of 1 lemon** or 1 teaspoon **vanilla extract** (optional)

2 tablespoons **brandy** (optional)

If using homemade, roll out each piece of phyllo dough (filo pastry) into a thin sheet. Brush a baking pan exactly the same size as the sheets of phyllo with melted butter. Alternatively, cut the sheets of phyllo to fit your baking pan and brush it with melted butter. Combine the nuts, cinnamon, and cloves in a bowl.

Preheat the oven to 350°F (180°C / Gas Mark 4).

Lay 4 sheets of phyllo on the base of the prepared baking pan, brushing each with melted butter. Sprinkle some of the nut mixture evenly over them. Continue layering the sheets of phyllo, 1 at a time and brushing each with melted butter, and sprinkling with some of the nut mixture until all of it has been used and only 4 sheets of phyllo remain. (If it has been necessary to trim the phyllo, brush the trimmings with melted butter and place between the layers.) Top with the remaining sheets of phyllo, brushing each one with melted butter. Score the top layers with a sharp knife into small diamond-shaped or triangular pieces. Stick a clove in the center of each piece, if you like. Brush with the remaining melted butter and sprinkle lightly with warm water to prevent the phyllo from curling. Bake for 30–40 minutes, or until golden brown.

Meanwhile, make the syrup. Put the sugar, corn syrup or honey, and lemon zest or vanilla extract, if using, into a small pan. Pour in 2 cups (450 ml / 16 fl oz) water and bring to a boil, stirring constantly until the sugar has dissolved. Simmer, without stirring, for 5 minutes. Stir in the brandy, if using, and remove from the heat. Ladle the hot syrup carefully and evenly over the baklava as soon as you take it out of the oven. Let it absorb the syrup and cool completely. Baklava keeps, covered loosely with a cloth, at room temperature for 1–2 weeks.

Nut Pastry Pinwheels

Makes 16–18 pinwheels
Preparation time 1 hour
Cooking time 40 minutes

½ cup (120 ml / 4 fl oz) melted **clarified butter**, plus extra for brushing

3 cups (350 g / 12 oz) **walnuts**, coarsely ground

2 teaspoons **ground cinnamon**

1 teaspoon **ground cloves**

9 oz (250 g) ready-made **phyllo dough** (filo pastry)

FOR THE SYRUP

1½ cups (300 g / 11 oz) **superfine (caster) sugar**

1 tablespoon freshly squeezed **lemon juice**

4 tablespoons **corn syrup** or **liquid glucose**

Preheat the oven to 350°F (180°C / Gas Mark 4) and brush 1 or 2 cookie sheets (baking trays) with melted butter. Combine the ground walnuts, cinnamon, and cloves in a bowl.

Stack 3 phyllo sheets, one on top of the other, brushing each with melted butter. Sprinkle some of the walnut mixture over the surface and lay another 2 sheets of phyllo on top, brushing each with melted butter. Sprinkle with a little more of the walnut mixture and lay another 2 phyllo sheets on top, brushing each with melted butter. Repeat the procedure once more.

Starting at the short end, roll up tightly into a thick cylinder. Dampen the edge and press to seal. Using a sharp knife, cut the cylinder into 1½-inch (4-cm) slices. Put the pinwheels on the prepared cookie sheet, side by side, cut sides up. Make more pinwheels in the same way with the remaining phyllo. Brush the tops with the remaining melted butter and bake for about 40 minutes, or until golden brown.

Meanwhile, make the syrup. Put the sugar, lemon juice, and corn syrup or glucose into a pan, pour in 1½ cups (350 ml / 12 fl oz) water, and bring to a boil, stirring until the sugar has dissolved. Boil, without stirring, for 5 minutes, then remove from the heat. Ladle the syrup over the pinwheels as soon as they are removed from the oven. Let them absorb the syrup and cool completely. Transfer to a serving dish. They keep well uncovered at room temperature for 1–2 weeks.

Kataifi Pastry Rolls

▼

Makes 15–18 rolls
Preparation time 1 hour
Cooking time 1 hour

2¼ cups (250 g / 9 oz) **walnuts**, chopped

2 tablespoons **rusk crumbs**

1 tablespoon **ground cinnamon**

1 teaspoon grated **lemon zest**

1 teaspoon **ground cloves**

1 tablespoon **brandy**

9 oz (250 g) **kataifi pastry**

1 cup (250 ml / 8 fl oz) melted **clarified butter**, plus extra for brushing

chopped **pistachio nuts**, to decorate

FOR THE SYRUP

3 cups (600 g / 1 lb 5 oz) **superfine (caster) sugar**

4 tablespoons **corn syrup** or **liquid glucose**

1 **cinnamon stick** or 1 teaspoon grated **lemon zest**

Combine the chopped walnuts, rusk crumbs, cinnamon, lemon zest, and cloves in a bowl and sprinkle with the brandy.

Fluff up the kataifi and divide it into 15–18 pieces. Cover with a damp dish towel while you are working, as it dries quickly. Tease out 1 section into a 4 × 8-inch (10 × 20-cm) strip. Put 1 tablespoon of the nut mixture at one end and roll up loosely. Make more rolls in the same way.

Preheat the oven to 350°F (180°C / Gas Mark 4) and brush a baking pan with melted butter. Arrange the rolls in the prepared pan and drizzle the melted butter evenly over them. Cover the pan with aluminum foil and bake for 30 minutes. Remove the foil and bake for 30 minutes more, or until crisp and golden.

Meanwhile, make the syrup. Put the sugar, corn syrup or glucose, and cinnamon stick or lemon zest into a pan. Pour in 2 cups (450 ml / 16 fl oz) water and bring to a boil, stirring until the sugar has dissolved. Boil, without stirring, for 5 minutes, then remove from the heat and discard the cinnamon. Carefully ladle the syrup over the rolls, letting them absorb it before adding more. Let cool, then sprinkle with chopped pistachios. Keep uncovered at room temperature for 1–2 weeks.

Sour Cherries in Syrup

Makes 2¼ lb (1 kg)
Preparation time 24 hours (including standing and cooling)
Cooking time 45 minutes

2¼ lb (1 kg) **sour cherries**

5 cups (1 kg / 2¼ lb) **superfine (caster) sugar**

½ teaspoon **citric acid** or 2 tablespoons freshly squeezed **lemon juice**

½ cup (120 ml / 4 fl oz) **corn syrup** or **liquid glucose**

Pour ½ cup (120 ml / 4 fl oz) water into a bowl. Using a cherry pitter (stoner), remove the pits (stones) from the cherries, working over a bowl to catch the juice. Drop the pits into the water, stir, and drain over the cherries into another bowl. Make alternating layers of the cherries and sugar in a heavy pan, pour in the juice, cover, and let stand overnight.

The next day, set the pan over low heat and gradually bring to a boil. Increase the heat and boil, stirring occasionally and skimming off any scum that rises to the surface, for 35 minutes. Reduce the heat, add the citric acid or lemon juice and corn syrup or glucose, and simmer, stirring occasionally, until setting point is reached. To test for setting, dip a tablespoon into the syrup and hold it vertically, letting the syrup drip back into the pan. Let the final drops drip over a small dish. If they hold their shape and remain intact, the syrup has set. On a candy (sugar) thermometer, setting point is reached when it registers 220°F (105°C).

Remove from the heat and let cool, shaking the pan several times to help the fruit absorb syrup and plump up. Carefully ladle into sterilized jars, seal, label, and store in a cool, dark place, or in the refrigerator.

Quinces Baked in Wine with Yogurt

Serves 6
Preparation time 15 minutes
Cooking time 1 hour 40 minutes

2¼ lb (1 kg) **quinces**

2 tablespoons freshly squeezed **lemon juice**

2 cups (450 ml / 16 fl oz) **sweet red wine**

10 **cloves**

2 **cinnamon sticks**

1½ cups (300 g / 11 oz) **superfine (caster) sugar**

2¼ cups (500 ml / 18 fl oz) strained plain or thick **Greek yogurt**, to serve

Preheat the oven to 350°F (180°C / Gas Mark 4).

Rub the quinces to remove the fuzz on the skin, rinse, and cut into quarters. Remove the cores, put the pieces of fruit into a baking dish, and sprinkle with the lemon juice.

Put the cores into a pan with the wine, cloves, and cinnamon, cover, and simmer for 10 minutes. Strain and reserve the wine.

Sprinkle the quinces with the sugar and reserved wine, cover with aluminum foil, and bake for 1 hour. Remove the aluminum foil, turn the pieces of quince over, and reduce the oven temperature to 225°F (110°C / Gas Mark ¼) and bake for 30 minutes more, until they are well glazed with the wine sauce. Serve hot or cold with the yogurt.

Almond "Pears"

Makes 80 "pears"
Preparation time 14 hours (including standing, cooling, and drying)
Cooking time 15–20 minutes

9 cups (1 kg / 2¼ lb) **almonds**, blanched and finely ground

5 tablespoons **coarse semolina**, plus extra for sprinkling

2½ cups (500 g / 1 lb 2 oz) **superfine (caster) sugar**

4 tablespoons **rosewater**, plus extra for dipping

3 tablespoons **honey**

½ teaspoon **almond extract**

80 whole **cloves**

confectioners' (icing) sugar, for coating

Combine the ground almonds, semolina, sugar, and rosewater in a bowl and knead into a smooth, pliable paste that holds its shape. Cover with a dish towel and let stand overnight.

The next day, knead the paste, gradually incorporating the honey and almond extract. If the paste is too stiff and dry, add a little more rosewater.

Preheat the oven to 350°F (180°C / Gas Mark 4). Line a cookie sheet (baking tray) with baking parchment and sprinkle with semolina. Shape small pieces of the marzipan into pears and insert 1 clove in the top of each for a stalk. Put the pears onto the prepared cookie sheet and bake for 15–20 minutes. Let cool on a wire rack.

Dip quickly in rosewater and roll in confectioners' (icing) sugar to coat. Let dry for 1–2 hours, then roll in confectioners' sugar again so that they are thickly coated and white.

Note: These almond treats made on Hydra, Spetses, and Andros are often served at christenings. A tiny bow, pink for girls and blue for boys, is pinned to the top of each pear with a clove.

Index

Index

O

P

Q

R

Recipe Notes

Butter should always be unsalted, unless otherwise specified.

All herbs are fresh, unless otherwise specified.

Eggs are medium (US large), unless otherwise specified.

Individual vegetables and fruits, such as onions and apples, are assumed to be medium, unless otherwise specified.

All milk is whole (3% fat), homogenized, and lightly pasteurized, unless otherwise specified.

All salt is fine sea salt, unless otherwise specified.

Exercise a high level of caution when following recipes involving any potentially hazardous activity, including the use of high temperatures, open flames and when deep-frying. In particular, when deep-frying add food carefully to avoid splashing, wear long sleeves and never leave the pan unattended.

Cooking times are for guidance only. If using a fan (convection) oven, follow the manufacturer's instructions concerning the oven temperatures.

All herbs, shoots, flowers and leaves should be picked fresh from a clean source. Do exercise caution when foraging for ingredients, which should only be eaten if an expert has deemed them safe to eat. In particular, do not gather wild mushrooms yourself before seeking the advice of an expert who has confirmed their suitability for human consumption. As some species of mushrooms have been known to cause allergic reaction and illness, do take extra care when cooking and eating mushrooms and do seek immediate medical help if you experience a reaction after preparing or eating them.

Exercise caution when making fermented products, ensuring all equipment is spotlessly clean, and seek expert advice if in any doubt.

When no quantity is specified, for example of oils, salts and herbs used for finishing dishes, quantities are discretionary and flexible.

All spoon and cup measurements are level, unless otherwise stated. 1 teaspoon = 5 ml; 1 tablespoon = 15 ml. Australian standard tablespoons are 20 ml, so Australian readers are advised to use 3 teaspoons in place of 1 tablespoon when measuring small quantities.

Cup, metric and imperial measurements are used in this book. Follow one set of measurements throughout, not a mixture, as they are not interchangeable.

Author Biography

Vefa Alexiadou was the leading authority on Greek cookery, and a tireless advocate for preserving Greek culinary traditions, serving on the board of the Centre for the Preservation of Traditional Greek Gastronomy. With her own television series in Greece, and regular appearances on international shows, such as *The Martha Stewart Show*, she shared authentic Greek cuisine with a worldwide audience. She is a best-selling author of thirteen books, including the critically acclaimed *Greece: The Cookbook*, published by Phaidon in 2017.

Phaidon Press Limited
2 Cooperage Yard
London E15 2QR

Phaidon Press Inc.
111 Broadway
New York, NY 10006

Phaidon SARL
55, rue Traversière
75012 Paris

phaidon.com

First published 2026

ISBN 978 1 83729 156 4

The recipes in this book are from *Vefa's Kitchen*, with the exception of page 40 which is from *The Greek Vegetarian Cookbook* by Heather Thomas. The first English edition of *Vefa's Kitchen* was published by Phaidon in 2009.

A CIP catalogue record for this book is available from the British Library and the Library of Congress.

Commissioning Editor: Emilia Terragni
Project Editor: Rachel Malig
Production Controller: Gary Hayes
Design: Gabrielle Guy
Photography: Edward Park; cover photograph/page 41 by Haarala Hamilton.

Printed in China

The publishers would like to thank Hilary Bird, Julia Hasting, João Mota, Ellie Smith, Tracey Smith, and Kathy Steer for their contributions to the book.